THE STORY OF MAIDSTONE ZOO

Ann Hayes

December 1995

The author and the lion, 1951.

The Story of
Maidstone Zoo

Vickie Harris

MERESBOROUGH BOOKS
1994

ISBN 0948193 808

Published for the author by
Meresborough Books
17 Station Road, Rainham, Kent, ME8 7RS

Typeset in 10 pt. Plantin and printed by
Harris Printers, Milton Road, Sittingbourne, Kent

Introduction

Maidstone Zoo at Cobtree Park was the creation of Hugh Garrard Tyrwhitt-Drake, who was a remarkable man by any standard: zoologist, writer, artist, business man, many times Mayor of Maidstone, and finally High Sheriff of Kent.

His Zoo gave pleasure to hundreds of thousands of people over a period of more than a quarter of a century, and is today remembered with affection by many, some young when Tyrwhitt-Drake opened it, others young when he closed it, and others again who worked in it.

It is for all of these people that I wrote this book, which has been over ten years in the making. When I began, I approached the late Lady Edna Tyrwhitt-Drake, who was most kind, for assistance; but I learned from her that all of the papers and records of the Zoo had been lost.

I have therefore had to search for my facts in libraries and newspaper files, and in the recollections of everyone I could find who had been associated in any way with the Zoo. Some people I met, some I telephoned, and to others I wrote. It is impossible to name them all, but I should like to thank everyone who helped me, and particularly to mention Mrs. Enid Simmonds, Mrs. Thelma Cornelius, Mr. Martin Hammond and Mr. John Edwards.

My very special thanks are reserved for Denis Hayes, without whose editing skills this book would never have been published. His selfless enthusiasm for the task earns my undying gratitude.

Inevitably, there is much that is missing in the story, and a few facts may be wrongly recorded. I have not, for example, been able to find reliable details of the veterinary surgeons who advised Sir Garrard, nor of all the variations in the prices of animals which took place during the Zoo's existence.

People's names, too, have been a source of difficulty at times. It may be that some of them have been spelt incorrectly, and if this is so, I apologise to those concerned, and to their families.

I also apologise to any who played a part in the Cobtree story and whose names have been omitted altogether. It was not deliberate; but in the end memories of events long past can play false and so, in the absence of any formal records, there are almost certain to be mistakes and oversights. If you can tell me of any, please do; I will see that corrections are made in future editions.

Vickie Harris

Sir Garrard Tyrwhitt-Drake, Kt, J.P., D.L., F.Z.S.

The Early Years

HUGH GARRARD TYRWHITT-DRAKE, always known as Garrard, was born in Maidstone on 22nd May, 1881. The origin of the Tyrwhitt-Drake family is lost in the mists of time: they have been landowners, farmers and clergymen in many parts of the country, and the name crops up among early Members of Parliament. Garrard's father, Hugh William, came from Buckinghamshire to Maidstone, where he lived initially in the London Road area. He seems to have been the first member of the family to go into trade, entering into partnership with Mr. A. F. Style to form the the brewing business of A. F. Style & Company, which later became Style & Winch Ltd. He moved to Cobtree Manor, a large country house standing in extensive grounds surrounded by orchards, in 1896.

Garrard's first lessons came from a governess, who was followed by a tutor, Mr. Bartlett, who lived at Ditton. At the age of ten Garrard was sent to a preparatory school at Hastings, and from there he went on to Charterhouse. He does not seem to have enjoyed life there; although he was a good horseman, he had little aptitude or interest in other sports, and by his own account, was no great scholar. Despite this, in later life he won international renown as a Zoologist as well as pursuing a successful business career and revealing considerable talent as both a writer and an artist.

During his life he wrote three books, "Beasts and Circuses" which was published in 1936, "My Life with Animals" which came out in 1939, and "The English Circus and Fairground" issued in 1946. In addition, for many years from 1912 onwards he was the Editor of the Year Book of the Amateur Menagerie Club. He designed and painted many inn signs for the family brewing business, habitually produced his own Christmas cards, often featuring comic animals, and frequently embellished his personal letters with animal illustrations. During the Great War his medical

Cobtree Manor.

drawings were good enough to be studied by senior officers of the Royal Army Medical Corps, and in the zoo he was later to set up at Cobtree his talent as a mural painter and signwriter was put to frequent use.

From an early age Garrard was fascinated by wild animals. When still very young, he was given a model zoo, and playing with it soon began to develop the seriousness of purpose which set the pattern of his later life. Every morning and evening he meticulously "fed" his model animals and cleaned out their cages, and he used his pocket-money to add to his collection. When only six years old he was given some Leghorn chickens, in the keeping of which he soon became an expert. He joined the local Poultry Club, and soon began to show his birds at events in both Great Britain and on the continent, winning many medals and certificates. He continued to play a leading role in the Poultry Club's affairs for many years, and for a time was active at a national level, becoming Secretary of the Poultry Club of Great Britain.

From the day of his first visit Garrard loved the circus. Often as a small boy he persuaded his father to allow him to go several times to the same circus while it was in town, and his fascination with the Big Top never waned. In his twenties and thirties he sometimes went on what he called a holiday with the famous circus of Lord John Sanger. Typically, he would spend two weeks on the road, having no holiday in the common meaning of the word, but working hard with regular members of the staff, mucking-out, fly-posting, undertaking front-of-house duties, or whatever else needed to be done. No doubt the circus animals were part of the appeal, for Garrard's interest in wildlife had grown steadily with the years, encouraged by the many visits to London Zoo on which he was taken while still young.

In 1899 Garrard left Charterhouse, and his father sent him to Argentina to spend a year on a ranch owned by friends of the family. A spell abroad before proceeding to Oxford or Cambridge was thought to widen a young man's horizon, and was a frequent feature of the upbringing of the wealthy young at the time — although usually the destination was Europe, not South America.

The trip put what was perhaps the final seal on Tyrwhitt-Drake's interest in wild animals, an interest which was never to leave him for the rest of his life. His father may well not have foreseen, however, that when he returned, young Garrard would bring with him a puma cub and a young viscacha — a small rodent peculiar to South America. These rather unlikely companions were housed in a hut adjoining the house at Cobtree Manor. They were the foundation of what grew into the largest private collection of animals in England, and ultimately into a major regional zoo.

Following his return to England, Tyrwhitt-Drake started work in the office of Style & Winch, his father's firm. He then moved on to gain practical experience at Fox's Brewery at Green Street Green, and returned to the family business in 1903. Meanwhile he made a number of additions to his animal collection which grew into a small menagerie; and in 1907 he purchased his first large mammal, a Canadian bear which he obtained from a dealer in the East End of London. Gentlefolk rarely, if ever, penetrated the East End at that time, and Garrard took his father with him to clinch the deal. In later life, he always maintained that of all wild animals, the Canadian bear was the most deadly.

The following year his father died, but Garrard continued to purchase large animals, and by 1910 had the second largest private collection in England. In 1912 he became a Director of Style & Winch, and at the same time was appointed Manager of the Bottling Department. Meanwhile, he had started to open his menagerie from 2.30 to 4.30 on Wednesday afternoons — early closing day in Maidstone. He charged 6d. (2½p) for admission, and after a while began to donate the receipts to West Kent General Hospital.

In 1912 he was elected to Maidstone Borough Council and began a lifetime of public service; he was twelve times Mayor, the first time in 1915, became a Magistrate in 1926, was made a Freeman of the Borough in 1930, and was appointed Alderman in 1934. In 1945 he became Deputy Lieutenant of the County, and the culmination of his public life came in 1956, when he was appointed High Sheriff of Kent.

A portrait of Tyrwhitt-Drake as a young man with an African lioness.

By 1913 Garrard had the largest private collection of animals in England. Included were six lions, four bears, eight wolves, two camels and a vulture, as well as sheep, goats and birds. In June however the open days at Cobtree ceased: months of negotiation had come to a successful conclusion, and all the livestock was caged or crated. On 11th July the entire collection was taken by train to Edinburgh, loaned to the Scottish Zoological Society as the nucleus of its new Zoo until the Society could build up its own animal stocks. This it appears to have succeeded in doing by October, for it is recorded that the animals then returned to Cobtree.

Early the following year, Tyrwhitt-Drake, who had meanwhile become a Fellow of the Zoological Society of London, formed a private company to set up a zoo at Tovil Court, an empty mansion standing in some fifteen acres of grounds a few miles from Cobtree Manor. It was at this time that George Thorneycroft, later to become his Head Keeper, joined him. Garrard seems to have done most of the organising of the new zoo and the preparation of the cages and paddocks himself, and in the Spring, some 250 animals, mostly from Cobtree, were moved in; but, unfortunately, disagreement broke out among the Directors over the question of Sunday opening, to which one was adamantly opposed. The outbreak of the First World War adding to the difficulties, it was decided in October to wind up the company and close the zoo.

Garrard's animals returned to Cobtree Manor, where problems caused by the war soon made themselves felt. By the summer of 1915 he had lost all his keepers except for a 73 year old ex-carter and a lady wild animal trainer from Belgium, and it became urgently necessary to reduce the animal stock. Fortune favoured him and he managed to sell a large collection, ranging from lions to parrots, to the Bronx Zoo in New York. In June he sailed to America with the animals on the steamship Minnehaha, and after safely delivering them returned to England unaccompanied on the Lapland. The trip was his first break from routine for several years, and he treated it as a holiday.

The urge to collect had not left him however. Even while he was disposing of a large part of his collection, he added to it his first specimen of the world's largest land mammal. Jumbo the elephant had been purchased as a baby in 1912 by the Daily Mirror newspaper, and for two years toured the country, promoting the paper and raising funds for local charities. Then, in 1914, he was presented to the London Zoological Society, and went on display in Regents Park Zoo. His stay there was short-lived, however, for after a few months Tyrwhitt-Drake made an offer for him which was accepted, and on 26th March, before the exodus to New York, Garrard arrived at the London Zoo to collect him. Sadly, Jumbo's life at Cobtree Manor was also brief, for he contracted pneumonia and died there in 1916.

Despite the war, in the winter of 1915 The World Fair was held at Islington, and Tyrwhitt-Drake secured a contract to supply the organisers with "ten wagons with animals", the varieties being unclear. They must have been pleased with the selection, however, for he continued to provide the livestock for the show, an amalgam of fun-fair, circus and menagerie which continued after the war, until 1929.

Garrard was now well established in public life, and as the war dragged on, he was appointed Liaison Officer between the farmers of the district and the Commanding Officers of four Labour Corps. He was not called up himself because of his medical grade, but volunteered for service in the Veterinary Corps, and in 1917 was directed to the Hospital for Sick Mules in Wales. Here he tended animals in cold, damp conditions which would have taxed a man in first class health.

Fortunately for him, the corporal in charge of the dispensary was almost 60 years old, and after a short time received his discharge. As Garrard understood Latin and could thus read the prescriptions, he was given the corporal's job. In his new position, he put his talent as an artist

An example of Tyrwhitt-Drake's artistic talent.

to good use, making water-colour sketches of the more interesting and unusual injuries and ailments encountered among the hospital's patients. Many of these found their way to Corps H.Q., where they aroused considerable interest.

In the Spring of 1918 Garrard asked for a transfer to the Labour Corps. This was granted, and he returned to Kent. The end of the war found him driving a tractor on a farm near Canterbury. He was discharged early in 1919, and by the summer he was back in the animal business.

When George Thorneycroft came back from the war, Tyrwhitt-Drake appointed him his Head Keeper; and as other old members of his staff began to return, Garrard went into partnership with a man named David Taylor, with whom he organised a small tenting show. In 1920 a third man, John Swallow, joined the partnership, and the three men organised a large and successful travelling exhibition; but by the following year the partnership had come to an end and Tyrwhitt-Drake was working alone. He put on his own menagerie show in 1921, and from then until 1933 in every summer organised at least one, at Southend, Crystal Palace or Margate. One year he ran three simultaneously.

The 1921 show included a circus, which he set up in the grounds of the Kursaal in Southend; but competition from the already existing fun-fair was strong, and the venture was not very successful. Nothing daunted, in July he moved the entire operation to Margate, and there it did much better.

In 1922 he achieved a lifetime's ambition, opening his own travelling circus. At Easter that year Garrard's Royal Circus pitched tent for the first time at Headcorn, and during the following summer it travelled successfully as far afield as the Isle of Wight. But he was now fully employed in the family business, and the extent of his public duties was increasing; regretfully he found that he could not devote enough time to the circus to ensure its continued success. So the achievement of this dream was short-lived, and in 1923 he set himself a more modest target: a small resident circus at the Crystal Palace. This was well received, and after its planned run, moved for a ten-day season to the Albert Hall where it performed for the benefit of Lord Mayor Treloar's Hospital for Blind Children.

Encouraged by his success, Tyrwhitt-Drake decided to add a menagerie to the circus, and ran combined circus and menagerie shows in aid of local hospitals in Maidstone Agricultural Hall, of which he obtained the use rent free, in the winters of 1924, 1925, 1926, 1928 and 1930. The hospitals benefited by amounts ranging from £500 to £1,000 — considerable amounts at that time. Nor was this Garrard's only contribution to local good causes. In the summer of 1928 he took Nero, one of his lions, to several fêtes held in support of local charities. Nero was housed in a specially built cage, which would be towed to the venue by a lorry. On arrival at the site, a canvas enclosure, large enough to accommodate about 100 spectators, would be erected. Admission to the enclosure cost 3d. (1¼p) for adults and 2d. for children, and Tyrwhitt-Drake would entertain the audience from inside the cage, talking about lions in general and Nero in particular, while Nero ambled round, and sometimes rubbed himself against his owner like a cat.

Meanwhile, in 1925 at the age of 44, Tyrwhitt-Drake had married. The wedding was at Boxley Church, and his bride, Miss Edna Mary Vine, was considerably younger than he. One of her grandfathers was a leading cleric in Norfolk, her father the proprietor of a hairdressing business in Week Street, Maidstone. She was supportive of all his activities, but did not share his overwhelming interest in animals.

During the late twenties, Garrard had not only the responsibilities of married life to consider, but also more demanding duties at Style & Winch, where he had become the firm's Wine and Spirit Buyer. In addition, he had been appointed a Director of the Maidstone Waterworks Company, and as well as being a member of the London Zoological Society was a corresponding member of the Zoological Societies of Ireland and New York and of many other organisations and learned societies: all this in addition to his membership of the Borough Council and the further duties which followed his appointment as a Justice of the Peace. As the thirties dawned, he decided that his lifestyle ought to become slightly less hectic.

There was another consideration. The cost of organising shows on rented sites far from home was becoming insupportable; indeed, the expense of maintaining his private animal collection, which had increased immensely in size, was itself becoming a serious burden. For a time Tyrwhitt-Drake considered disposing of perhaps as much as three-quarters of it; but in the end the decision proved one that he could not bear to take.

In 1932 the man always known as "Captain" Gates, although he held no military rank, joined his staff. Gates had been a shepherd on Romney Marsh until coming to Cobtree, and was first employed as a general stockman and gatekeeper. Later he became car park attendant, and finally elephant keeper. Living in the Lodge by the main gate, he stayed with Sir Garrard till he died. The following year, at the age of 52, unable to consider disposing of his animals, Tyrwhitt-Drake recalled the time, 20 years earlier, when he had loaned most of his stock to Edinburgh. He had learned a lot about running a public zoo then, and he realised that at Cobtree Manor he had all the pre-requisites for setting one up: a large, good quality collection of animals, plenty of room in the orchards surrounding the manor for expansion, and a site well-placed to attract visitors from a large area in Kent and East Sussex. He had been unable to sustain his early dream of running a travelling circus. Now the idea of running a zoo seemed a very fair alternative.

Once he had decided to take the plunge, Tyrwhitt-Drake set to work without delay, himself preparing the plans for the zoo, and then making an immediate start on the practical work of creating paddocks and building cages. He set aside an area of some ten acres for the initial development, at the same time preparing coach and car parks on both sides of the long, tree-lined drive which led from the Chatham Road to the manor house. A conveniently sited bus stop near the main gate would cater for those who lacked their own transport — which in 1933 meant the great majority of the zoo's potential customers. Between the vehicle parks and a second gate on the drive, Garrard erected a green painted pay box: this was over 500 yards from the entrance to the park, a long way for people to walk, but clearly not considered excessive at the time. The second gate, which gave access to the house and gardens, was about ten yards beyond the pay box, and between the two Tyrwhitt-Drake laid a footpath bearing off to the right, along which visitors to the zoo would be directed by signs; this path was the first facility to be completed. Then, using dozens of rolls of Ryland's "Crapo" galvanised wire fencing and chestnut hop-poles, he set up paddocks for the deer and other non-dangerous animals; and on a strip of concrete which had earlier formed the floor of some cow sheds, he lined up some of his travelling wagons, covered their wheels with wooden panels painted to represent a stone wall, and used them to house the lions and other dangerous beasts. To establish a centre of interest which could be readily identified he decided to group all the docile white animals together, and to do this, he set up a sectioned paddock for them, which he called The White Farmyard. At the same time he built cages for the monkeys, raccoons, jackals, dogs and foxes, and aviaries for the birds, which included

A view of the deer paddock, showing the Ryland's "Crapo" fencing which Tyrwhitt-Drake favoured, and, in the background, one of the keeper's bungalows.

Tyrwhitt-Drake's skill is displayed by these murals done by him on the outside walls of Children's Corner. Distorting mirrors added to the gaiety of the scene.

budgerigars, finches and parrots. Garrard's wife was very fond of these, and he set up a private collection for her. Not far from the manor he already had a bear house, and near to this was a facility which all zoos need, but which visitors rarely see, a slaughter-house.

Along the boundary of the estate which fronted Forstal Road, Garrard created a Children's Corner featuring many varieties of small and domesticated animals; he himself painted scenes from "Alice in Wonderland" on the rear walls of the cages. An ex-army hut was purchased and set up as a café serving lunches and teas and nearby a small kiosk was erected for the sale of sweets, animal foods, postcards and the like; and finally all the site facilities were linked by footpaths, prudently made, in case the zoo was not a success, by an extremely economical yet effective method.

The existing turf was cut to the desired width and the grass removed; the edges were lined with rough wooden boards, which were nailed to wooden pegs driven into the ground; and fine ash was then laid between the boards, raked and rolled. When the visitors began to arrive, they trod it down at no cost. Later Tyrwhitt-Drake improved the paths by spraying them with tar and topping them with sharp ballast. The end result was an effective and hardwearing surface which needed minimal maintenance.

A Dream Fulfilled

O N the afternoon of Monday, 29th March, 1934, Kent Zoo Park was opened. The ceremony was performed by Bertram Mills, the owner of a circus famous throughout the country, who was introduced to a large body of the great and the good, as well as many ordinary folk from the neighbourhood, by Alderman William Day, the Mayor of Maidstone. After the speeches, Garrard presented Mr. Mills with a bronze statuette of a lioness with two cubs, and the visitors were then taken on a conducted tour of the cages and enclosures. Almost all the preparatory work had been completed, and the guests, including a large press party, gained a good first impression of the new venture. After the tour, the great and the good went into the manor house to take tea with Garrard and his wife.

The Zoo's success was soon confirmed. The following Friday marked the start of the Easter holiday, which was then even more important to many people than it is now: it was the longest break that thousands had in the whole year. Over the four day period, more than 13,900 admission tickets were sold, and on Easter Monday no less than 300 cars were parked in the grounds, an extraordinary number in an age when car ownership was still the exception rather than the rule. The onslaught overwhelmed the Zoo's modest catering resources; but the visitors took the shortcomings in good part, and learning from experience, the facilities were quickly extended, so that such a situation should never occur again. It was from this surge of visitors that the first applications for membership of the Zoo Club were received. This was a body designed to provide for the interests of the more serious visitors to the Zoo, which Tyrwhitt-Drake had announced would be set up as soon as the Zoo opened. It continued to exist for several years, most of its meetings apparently taking place in a large shed which adjoined the lions wagons.

When the Zoo opened, it possessed a large collection of lions, two Malayan tigers named Rajah and Ranee, a laughing hyena known as

Tyrwhitt-Drake with some of his Mouflon sheep. The tit-bit basket he often carried is very visible.

Squeaks, a large polar bear called Trousers, a sloth bear christened Pauline and an Arabian camel named Baby, as well as numbers of American, Russian and Timber wolves, baboons, and green and rhesus monkeys. In addition, there were large collections of birds and smaller animals, some of them in the Children's Corner, which was an instant success. To see all these attractions cost 7d. (3p) for adults and 3d. (1¼p), for children under 12 — at first even less for those who belonged to a children's organisation called the Keg Megs, run by the Kent Messenger newspaper, and were wearing its badge when they bought their tickets. For them the prices were 5d. (2½p) for over twelves and 2d. for the under twelves.

Sadly, the promising start was marred after only a few weeks by a fatal accident. Frederick Cashford, a 16 year old assistant, had been clearing out the bear cage; as he finished, Tyrwhitt-Drake passed by and spoke to him. The lad had done his work passing a rake under the bars of the cage from the outside, for he was not authorised to enter the dangerous animals' enclosures. It was noticed that some debris remained uncleared inside the cage, and the boy attempted to remove them with the rake. However, they were out of reach, and Tyrwhitt-Drake told him to leave them: he would speak to Mr. Thorneycroft, and ask him to move the bear to her sleeping quarters, so that the litter could be taken out in safety. Tyrwhitt-Drake walked away and encountered Thorneycroft about 40 yards from the cage. They were discussing the problem when they heard screams and ran back to the cage, seizing sticks and a shovel as they went. They found Cashford outside the cage, but with his right arm through the bars and the fingers of his right hand gripped in the bear's teeth.

Desperate attempts were made from outside the cage to force the bear to release its grip, but without success, and seeing that Cashford's plight grew rapidly worse, Tyrwhitt-Drake hurried away to get more help. He quickly returned, accompanied by a groom and armed with an iron bar. Entering the cage, the two men finally beat the bear off, but not before the lad's right arm had been badly mauled, as well as his left hand, with which he had frantically tried to prise open the animal's mouth.

The boy was carried into the manor house, an ambulance was called, and the nurse who attended Tyrwhitt-Drake's mother gave first aid. But the ambulance seemed to be slow in coming, and it was decided to rush Cashford in one of the family cars to West Kent General Hospital. He arrived there in little more than ten minutes. It was soon found that the injuries he had suffered were very serious and an emergency operation to amputate his right arm above the elbow was carried out. The operation was initially successful but septicaemia set in, and on the last Sunday in April Cashford had a sudden relapse, and in the afternoon he died of heart failure.

An inquest was held in Maidstone the next day. Tyrwhitt-Drake told the coroner that the bear, a black Himalayan, had never previously shown aggressive tendencies during the three or four years during which he had owned it. Mr. Cashford, he said, had been in his employment since the previous October; one of his regular duties was the cleaning of the bear cage. He was not a venturesome lad, and Garrard was certain that he would not have been teasing the bear. He had, however, a tidy disposition, and it might have been that he stood on tiptoe, holding the bars of the cage with one hand, while trying to manœuvre the rake across the top; certainly the bear could not get its snout through the bars. The coroner said that no one would ever know exactly what had happened, and recorded a verdict of accidental death. The incident greatly upset Tyrwhitt-Drake, the more so because the publicity surrounding it attracted additional visitors to the

Zoo, drawn by morbid curiosity. The bear remained at the Zoo for many years, and was never again the source of any trouble.

Meanwhile, the other animals got on with their lives, peacefully indifferent to the lethal activities of the bear. A dingo (an Australian wild dog) gave birth to a litter of five puppies, and a baby lemur was born. Unfortunately, its father killed it before the staff knew of its arrival: lemurs very rarely breed in captivity, and no one had realised that the mother was pregnant.

At Whitsun a travelling fair, complete with swings, roundabouts, coconut-shies and side-shows, paid a visit, which further increased the tide of visitors, as did the completion of two new enclosures, the Goat Rock and the Sheep Rock. These featured a man made cliff-face, on which the mountain goats and sheep could leap from ledge to ledge as they would in the wild. Garrard had fine herds of goats and sheep, and large crowds would gather to admire their agility. In all, during the seven weeks from opening, no less than 28,000 people paid for admission to the Zoo, and 2,400 motorists used the car parks.

Goat Mountain and two of its inhabitants.

All through the summer the Zoo continued to prosper, until early in November Tyrwhitt-Drake closed it for the winter. Over 87,000 people had passed through the entrance gate since opening; his enterprise had paid off, and he decided to re-open in March and to use the intervening period to enlarge and further improve the facilities.

When the Zoo re-opened on 24th March, 1935, the area covered had grown to twelve acres, a reserve called Wolf Wood had been established, and near to this a small mammal house had been built containing twelve cages. The inhabitants included bonnet, mangabey, rhesus and other small monkeys, raccoons, which are about the size of cats and are common over much of North America, their near-relatives coatis, which are somewhat larger and have pig-like snouts, and agouties, a tail-less rodent about the size of a rabbit. The small mammal house operated on a one-way system: visitors entered at one end and emerged into Wolf Wood at the other.

The café had been extended and Mr. Beslee appointed Manager, and near to it a parrot house had been built. This was designed in the same way as the small mammal house, but with benches along each side of the interior, on which portable cages could be placed. Both buildings were heated by proprietory small slow burning coke stoves of the "Tortoise" brand, and were painted green, which had emerged as the Zoo's house colour and was generally used throughout from this time on.

The bears had also been provided with new quarters, large enclosures surrounded by thick metal bars embedded in a concrete floor, and in each a door at the rear leading to the animal's sleeping quarters. These backed onto the yard in which the bears had previously been located, which was now closed to the public. In all, at the start of the 1935 season, the Zoo contained no less than 130 enclosures and cages of varying kinds.

Among the most popular exhibits were Billy, a capybara or giant guinea pig, the largest species of rodent in the world, and Trousers the polar bear, who now had a pool in which to splash and laze. The Arabian camel also attracted many visitors; it had been moved from a shed to an open air enclosure with sleeping quarters at the rear. The camel liked the change, and so did the humans, for the fragrance in its old home had been memorable. Other favourites included some lion cubs which had been born in the Zoo the previous year.

Tyrwhitt-Drake's famous Royal Cream ponies were not technically part of the Zoo, but visitors had an excellent view of them as they walked along the drive from the main entrance, and also from inside the Zoo, for they roamed freely in the surrounding parkland. Garrard had built up a

May, Tyrwhitt-Drake's cream coloured mare, with some of the Royal Cream ponies.

large herd since purchasing his first stallion, named Prince, in 1913. He had been unable to find a cream mare to put to him, and so had tried a roan Shetland. This produced rather mixed results, so he experimented with Exmoor mares, some browns and one chestnut. Brown ponies were the outcome, but when in due course they were presented to Prince, pure cream ponies resulted every time.

They were lovely animals, well-mannered, intelligent and hardy, and were in great demand at Christmas time. For many years they could be seen pulling Cinderella's carriage — also supplied by Tyrhwitt-Drake, who had several in pantomimes of every grade, from the magnificent productions at the London Palladium down to modest shows at small local theatres. Prince and his offspring based their claim to the title "Royal" on the fact that two of his ancestors had been given to Queen Victoria by Lord George Sanger's Circus, which until 1911 was the line's only home, after she had admired them at a Royal Command performance. Subsequently she employed them to pull her bath-chair around the Royal gardens.

On Easter Monday, 1935, some 5,000 people visited the Zoo, with a corresponding demand for refreshments. This time, however, the catering department was prepared, and no cases of unsatisfied hunger or thirst were recorded. Many people brought picnics with them, and enjoyed al fresco meals among the cherry and apple blossom. Easter was late that year, and the park was looking at its loveliest for the holiday.

The parrot house drew large crowds: its collection of parrots, macaws and cockatoos included a number of individualists who soon became celebrities. There was a green Amazon called Lady who frequently urged "Polly, put the kettle on and we will all have tea", and a cockatoo who remarked, perhaps when Polly had put the kettle on, "Fourpence a pot". Another cockatoo was noted for his loud voice, and could always be heard above the clamour of birds and humans, bawling "What are you going to do?" At that time, colour photography was in its infancy and colour television had not been thought of, and the brilliant plumage of most of the birds surprised and thrilled visitors.

There were many births at Cobtree in May; they included six Royal Cream foals, three dingo pups, two fox cubs and two baby squirrels. An Upland goose from the Falkland Islands nested and laid four eggs, and from nearer home, two baby badgers found abandoned near Maidstone were brought in and soon settled down, quickly learning how to win titbits from admiring visitors.

Tyrwhitt-Drake was Mayor of Maidstone that year, and during the summer he invited the members of Kent County Council to visit the Zoo, and to take tea with him and Mrs. Tyrwhitt-Drake afterwards. Some fifty of them accepted the invitation, and after the regular Council meeting one Wednesday drove to Cobtree, where Garrard, a stickler for protocol, greeted them in his Mayoral robes. After the conducted tour, tea was served in the café, and the Councillors were surprised — or perhaps not, according to the state of their feet — to learn that while seeing the Zoo they had walked well over a mile.

In June the Zoo was presented with twenty shelduck eggs. Although the shelduck is commonly found along the estuaries of the Thames and the Medway — one of its favourite breeding grounds is the Isle of Grain — the Zoo had no resident ducks under which to incubate the eggs. So they were put under hens, who did not seem in the least put out, and by mid July sixteen ducks were successfully hatched. Two of the Upland geese also produced healthy chicks, and six Canada geese chicks were born at about the same time.

As the eggs were hatching, Garrard purchased a young chimpanzee named Martha. She travelled by boat from the Belgian Congo, now known as Zaire, to Rotterdam, and then set up a chimpanzee first by flying from

Martha the chimp enjoying an ice cream on a hot day.

Rotterdam to Croydon. The journey must have suited her, for she quickly settled down, and soon was often seen walking round the Zoo with Tyrwhitt-Drake as he made his regular tours of inspection. A South American llama was also added to the strength at this time; a beast of burden in her homeland, she was the first of her kind at Cobtree, although her relative the alpaca, bred for its wool, was already well established.

More new animals arrived as the summer progressed. One was a mature woolly monkey which had been a pet. His home had been Central or South America — probably the Upper Amazon — and he became a popular inmate with his coat of dense woolly fur and bullet head with what looked like a crew haircut. Other newcomers included twin cubs born to Ena, a lioness who herself had been born at Whipsnade and proved to be an excellent mother.

Visitors continued to flock to Cobtree, so much so that Tyrwhitt-Drake felt able to reduce the admission charges, which became 6d. (2½p) for adults and 3d. for children, a level at which they remained for several years. Members of the Kent Cycling Association were among the first to benefit from the new rates. Their second Annual Sports Day and Gymkhana (admission 2d., or rather less than 1p) was held in a field rented for the day at Cobtree, and many of the three or four hundred cyclists who took part visited the Zoo afterwards.

In September Garrard travelled to Sheringham in Norfolk, where the local Zoo was up for sale. Always eager to add good stock to his collection, he bought a pair of lions with a four month old cub to broaden his breeding base, as well as two blackfooted African penguins, an Amherst pheasant, a pair of Virginian eagle owls and an African pelican. He also purchased a Malayan porcupine and a Malayan bear, a type not previously seen at Cobtree. All the animals were quickly brought down to Kent, and went on show for the remainder of the season until the Zoo closed for the winter early in November.

The winter months, as always, were busy. Although the Zoo was closed, the animals demanded the same care and attention as in summer, while in addition to the usual maintenance and repair work, advantage was taken of the lull to add a number of new attractions.

Near the entrance to Wolf Wood a small aquarium was built, green painted in the now established house colours. It contained cold water fish such as rudd, roach and perch, which together with goldfish and orfe, could also be seen in the lake close to the drive. In addition there were tanks for tropical fish, which, to save heating costs, Garrard hired every summer from the London Zoo. Typically they included angel fish, rainbow fish and sword tails. When the Zoo re-opened, a small extra charge was made for a visit to the aquarium. An elephant house was also built; this

Gert and Daisy soon after their arrival.

was a sturdy wooden structure with a concrete base, and its first occupants were to be two young females ordered from Burma. Unfortunately they did not arrive in time for the opening of the 1936 season.

This took place on 22nd March. The ceremony was performed by the actress Fay Compton, already famous on stage and screen, and later known to a wider audience for her part in the TV production of "The Forsyte Saga". She was accompanied by her son Anthony Pelessier, and Owen Nares and his wife. The invited guests now had over one hundred and fifty cages and enclosures to inspect, as well as a substantial additional area of natural woodland which had been opened to the public. They saw Mitzi, the first baby monkey to be born at Cobtree for many years, and some young penguins, the first offspring of those purchased at Sheringham, as well as some fallow deer newly acquired from the Duke of Bedford.

The elephants ordered from Burma finally arrived in May, but turned out not to be precisely what Tyrwhitt-Drake had specified. Instead of a pair of three or four year olds each standing about four feet high, two six year olds appeared, about five feet six inches high and each weighing 1½ tons. This caused something of a problem: they had to be collected at once from the dockside, but the Zoo's lorry was not designed to cope with such loads. A solution was found, which worked, although it would certainly not be permitted today. Before it set out, extra wooden boards were fitted to the sides of the lorry, and once the animals had been persuaded to climb aboard, to the back as well. The vehicle then set out on a fraught journey back to Cobtree, which fortunately was accomplished without mishaps; and in due course the elephants were installed in their brand new home. Here a new difficulty at once became apparent. Someone had miscalculated the size to which Burmese elephants grow and the two newcomers, although only six years old, virtually filled the available accommodation, leaving them with no room for expansion. Consequently, very soon a new elephant house had to be built.

The young elephants settled down very quickly at Cobtree. Carl Fischer was engaged as their keeper and he taught them excellent manners, and also, to prevent them from becoming bored, some circus tricks, which they demonstrated from time to time. In addition, as they grew older he taught them to carry a howdah, and elephant rides (six people to a howdah) became a popular feature of visits to the Zoo. A ride cost 3d. for adults and 2d. for children.

In June the music hall and radio stars Elsie and Doris Waters, famous for their act featuring two charwomen named Gert and Daisy, came to

Cobtree to christen them. A large crowd attended the ceremony, at which Elsie and Doris poured Kent cider over the elephants' heads and fed them chunks of a tasty christening cake made from meal, bran, currants and bananas covered with sugar icing. Unsurprisingly, they were named Gert and Daisy.

Carl Fischer achieved some distinction among the Cobtree staff as being the only person ever known successfully to hoodwink Tyrwhitt-Drake over anything. In Fischer's case the trick involved the quantity of biscuits allegedly consumed by Gert and Daisy who seem to have seen rather fewer than Tyrwhitt-Drake paid for. He went on to become a famous international animal trainer, and died in West Berlin, many years later.

Garrard was Knighted in the Honours List that month: henceforth Sir Garrard. He drove to Buckingham Palace in his yellow Rolls Royce to receive the accolade "for public services", although as one of his friends commented, he would be best remembered for the work he did with animals. Thus he joined the small and select body of men and women to be honoured by King Edward VIII during his brief reign.

Soon after, a Dr. Cole of Benenden approached him with an unusual problem. He had been given a toucan, which is rather a large bird, and had nowhere to keep it. Would Sir Garrard like it as a gift? Sir Garrard would, and offered a generous quid pro quo: a day out at the Zoo for the Doctor and his family, and for all the schoolchildren of Benenden, with a fine tea to wind up the outing. They all came by bus and had a splendid day, being among the first visitors to see the Zoo's latest attraction, apart from the toucan itself. This was a black spider monkey from Cuba, a slender bodied animal with a very long tail which it uses as an extra hand. A denizen of tropical forests, it lives mainly on fruit, but if necessary will eat flowers and insects, and at a push, small birds and fish.

A few weeks later a visitor to the Zoo was slightly injured by one of the leopards. Mr. Harry Tester dropped some food in front of the animal's cage; as he stooped to pick it up, the leopard pushed a paw through the bars, clearly with the same idea in mind. Unfortunately the paw encountered not the food but Mr. Tester's hand. Luckily he suffered only slight injuries, and after treatment at West Kent General Hospital was able to go home.

Later in the same month a gentleman friend for Martha, previously a solitary chimpanzee, arrived from Leeds. About 3½ years old, he was named Albert, and suffered from a deformity of his left hand. Martha did not seem at all put out by this however, and took to him straight away: they became a popular couple, and often entertained visitors romping and wrestling round their cage.

In September three litters of lion cubs were born, and the Scottish Zoological Society presented Sir Garrard with a gannet, a sea bird rarely seen in the South of England. Another rare bird was purchased from the U.S.A.; this was a golden oriole, which is about the same size as a starling, but which has brilliant orange and black plumage. Among the visitors that month was Robertson Hare, a famous comedy actor of stage and screen,

The zoo train at Chatham Road station. A visitor is taking his ease on Jessie's footplate while the driver waits for the "right away".

who was mobbed by autograph hunters, and must have found it hard work actually to see the animals.

The Zoo closed for the winter at the beginning of November, and another programme of improvements and extensions was started. The most noticeable when the Zoo re-opened the following year was the miniature railway which Sir Garrard laid between the main entrance to Cobtree Manor and the pay kiosk. He purchased the track secondhand from a local quarry, and built simple stations, named Chatham Road and The Zoo, at each end. Wooden barriers were erected at both, so that access to the tarmac platforms could be controlled and queues organised at busy times. Avery Brothers of Maidstone built a steam-outline locomotive powered by a 14 hp petrol engine for the line, and two open eighteen seat coaches were constructed on the frames of old tram-cars, the original reversible seats being used. Mr. Avery himself often drove the engine, and at other times Ray Mitchell, Sir Garrard's chauffeur, was in charge. As well as being fun, a ride on the railway saved visitors the 500 yard walk from the main gate to the Zoo entrance for a modest fare inwards of 2d. adults, 1d. children, and outwards 1d. for everbody.

Two large lion pens were also built, with concrete floors and walls, and iron bars at the front. They were open to the sky, with covered sleeping quarters at the rear. Although larger than the converted travelling wagons in which the lions had previously been housed, the inmates did not appear to be either healthier or happier than before, and in fact did not seem to breed so freely. Sir Garrard believed that the animals did better in the wagons because, being off the ground, they were relatively free of draughts. Furthermore, having overall roofs, the wagons offered better shelter from sun and rain, and the wooden floors were probably warmer and more comfortable than concrete. At any rate, he never built any more concrete lion pens.

In addition, a model village was built, complete with houses, shops, a pub and a church. Named Cavey Village, and located near the White Farmyard, it became home to the Zoo's guinea-pigs. Some new animals were also added to the collection during the winter. They included the only Chinese tiger in Europe, a lively one year old which had been captured in Amoy when only ten days old and acquired by the crew of H.M.S. Kent while on station in the Far East. Known as Tiger Tim, he presented the mariners with something of a problem when they returned to Chatham, and they were relieved to find a good home for him at Cobtree.

Lady Edna with two lion cubs born in the Zoo.

Most years Sir Garrard entertained the press to lunch just before the new season; 1937 was no exception, and during his remarks he spoke of the successes already achieved, and of the tasks still confronting him. To ensure the viability of his Zoo, he said, something in the order of 120,000 visitors were necessary each season: and he thought that that figure was a reasonable target to aim for in the coming summer.

The opening ceremony was performed by Jessie Matthews, described at the time as having "an elegant streamlined chassis". She was accompanied by her husband Sonnie Hale, who had a completely different sort of chassis, and began by breaking a bottle of Kent champagne cider over the buffer-beam of the new railway engine and christening it "Jessie". She and Sonnie then went on to tour the Zoo with the other invited guests.

Among the new inmates they met were five cubs which had been born the previous year to Pauline, one of the eighteen lions now resident at Cobtree, Tiger Tim, who was now sixteen months old, and George, a Bengal tiger who hailed from Whipsnade. New from Oxford Zoo was a female leopard named Maharani, while a third tiger whose name and species is unrecorded had also been bought from Oxford Zoo. A Caucasian ibex or bearded goat was another newcomer whom Tiger Tim and his friends would no doubt have liked to meet, and near Wolf Wood a coypu or South American giant rat had produced a litter of five babies; this was the type of rat which in earlier times had been displayed in peep-shows as "The giant rat of the London sewers".

All the old favourites were still in residence, and admission charges for adults remained unchanged at 6d., though the price for children was increased to 4d. During the summer further inmates arrived, making a visit to Cobtree still better value. By July a two year old yak or grunting ox, and a three year old bison had joined the strength, and a small pond surrounded by mud and grass was being prepared for a seal which was expected in August. At the end of that month Sir Garrard was able to announce with justifiable pride that during the summer four of his lionesses had given birth to a total of twelve healthy cubs, an achievement which it was believed had never been equalled by any other British zoo.

In September another consignment of animals included, from Senegal, a rare pouched giant rat about twice the size of the common British rat, as well as a kinkajou from South America, a long tongued nocturnal animal more commonly known as a honey bear, and three prairie marmots, which Sir Garrard hoped would form the basis of a large colony such as already existed at Whipsnade. In addition, there were a pair of young emus and a male Canadian black bear, bought as a mate for the female already at Cobtree. All the new animals went on show within a few days of their arrival.

When the Zoo closed on 31st October, Sir Garrard was able to announce that over 110,000 people had paid for admission during the season — not quite the figure he had suggested in March, but nevertheless a good enough result to ensure its continued existence. With the Zoo now covering a considerable area, and with good housing provided for all its animals, the winter work programme was mainly confined to repainting and refurbishing the existing facilities. However, new houses for antelope and zebra were built and an additional tropical fish tank was added to the aquarium.

Comedian Claude Dampier performed the opening ceremony for the 1938 season. He was accompanied by Billy Carlyle and other celebrities, and entertained the crowd with some knock-about acts which went down very well. His turn with the elephants Gert and Daisy was a particular success: at one point he tried making a trunk telephone call using Daisy's tail by mistake, with results that had the audience rolling with laughter. At the end of the now customary tour of the Zoo, the visitors had the also now customary tea at the Manor with Sir Garrard and Lady Edna.

During the relatively quiet winter, Carl Fischer had taught Gert and Daisy some new routines, which attracted appreciative crowds from the start of the season. One of the most popular featured Fischer lying calmly on the ground while Gert or Daisy appeared to rest one of their feet on his nose. There were also some new animals to admire. One was a brindled gnu, a type of African antelope often known as a blue wildebeeste: it has the colour of a blue roan horse, the head of a buffalo, the body and legs of an antelope and the mane and tail of a mule. There were also some peccaries from South America, tail-less miniature wild pigs standing only some 14 inches high. And the display of tropical fish proved very popular.

The view from inside the bars of the new concrete lion cages.

There was a growing interest among the public in keeping tropical fish at home, and the staff at Cobtree were kept busy answering questions about the technicalities of the hobby.

The attendance over the Easter Holidays broke all previous records, over 15,000 people paying for admission. The café, which could now serve meals for up to 300 people, and nearby kiosk, were both kept on the run almost continuously, although many visitors brought their own food. Seats had been placed in many locations throughout the Zoo, and there were plenty of attractive, grassy areas where families could enjoy a picnic: the lawn in front of the lion cages was a particularly popular spot.

In May an orphan just three years old and 3 feet 6 inches tall arrived at Tilbury Docks on the steamship Salween from Rangoon. She was Ma Chaw (which is Burmese for Miss Darling), the smallest and one of the youngest elephants ever to arrive in England. She had made the long journey in the care of the ship's carpenter, who must have been truly devoted to her, for she was a demanding little creature. She required feeding six times a day, her diet consisting of a mixture of ground boiled rice, Quaker oats, maize flakes, brown sugar and fifty drops of halibut liver oil, the whole mixed in six tins of full cream condensed milk. In addition she took oranges and bananas for dessert, and when she arrived at Cobtree enjoyed some lettuce and cut grass as well. She was housed in a large hut (later used as the tack store) adjoining the lions' cages, which was warm and fairly draught free; it is thought that an extra charge was made for seeing her.

She stood the sea voyage to England very well, partly no doubt because of the care the carpenter had lavished on her, and soon settled down in the home Sir Garrard had offered her, appearing to enjoy the interest which she at once attracted. In July Gracie Fields came to Cobtree and in front of an audience of 10,000 poured a bottle of Kent champagne cider over Ma Chaw's head and christened her Sally. Afterwards Gracie delighted the crowd with some songs, "Sally" naturally being one of them, before retiring to the Manor for tea.

Later in the month, H.M.S. Emerald docked at Chatham carrying a pair of lion cubs which the ship's company presented to Sir Garrard. He was delighted, for he was always glad to bring new blood into his breeding stock. Cobtree had an outstanding reputation in this repect, particularly in lion breeding, which was carried on under the supervision of George Thorneycroft.

August saw an entirely new development: the main cages were floodlit, and fairy lights were hung among the trees along the footpaths. On Wednesdays and Sundays the Zoo remained open until 10.00 or 10.30 in the evening, and visitors could see the animals and the park in — literally — a new and attractive light. None of the animals appeared to object to the innovation except Albert the chimp, who clearly regarded unpaid overtime as an afront to his dignity, and retired to his sleeping quarters as soon as the lights came on.

The floodlighting was not repeated the following year, however; perhaps it was found to be too expensive, or maybe it was considered dangerous. Then war came, and floodlighting was of course out of the question. Afterwards, sadly, the experiment was never repeated.

Parties, particularly of children, were always welcomed at Cobtree, and at the end of August 400 children of members of the Maidstone branch of the British Legion visited the Zoo. They had an exciting day, rides on the railway and the elephants being among the highlights in the programme, while the acrobatics of the monkeys and chimpanzees were also much appreciated. And of course, all the children assembled to watch the feeding of the lions and tigers.

This took place at 4.00 p.m. daily except on Mondays (this because lions in the wild do not eat every day) a bell being rung ten minutes earlier to warn visitors that the spectacle was about to start. A trolley (a former milk cart) laden with raw meat was pushed along the front of the cages by a keeper while another walked ahead with a long two-pronged fork, which he used to push lumps of the meat into each cage through a gap at the bottom of the bars.

In September the Camping Club of Great Britain and a number of other organisations interested in outdoor activities held a rally in the grounds at Cobtree, with speeches and sports in which everyone could take part, and a combined admission fee for rally and Zoo of 9d. (3¾p). And in October, as the season neared its end, a baby llama, the first for 20 years, was born, and a rhesus monkey also gave birth to a healthy infant.

New animals purchased for the collection in the closing weeks of the season included a pair of African leopards, a pair of vultures and two black cuckoos; they joined existing inmates, many of which had acquired names without ever being formally christened. There was Stinkie the goat, for example, and Winnie the emu, as well as Big Bill the bison, Joey the penguin, and Cocky the cockatoo, who lived in Pets' Corner and frequently urged visitors to "give us a kiss". He also often enquired solicitously if they had had their breakfast.

By closing day, 55,000 people had visited Sally since her arrival five months earlier; over 375,000 people had visited the Zoo in four years, 60,000 people had ridden the railway. And, an indication of the growth in private motoring, more than 12,000 cars had parked in the Zoo's car park during the summer.

During the winter a number of new facilities were built. These included a new home for Gert and Daisy, in which this time due allowance was made for growth. The building was a large concrete structure, set close to the other elephant house. The cage was fronted with thick iron bars, in front of which there was a narrow walkway for staff, and then a waist high barrier of wood and chain link netting.

A bored lion in one of the ex-circus cages. The painted "stonework" with which Sir Garrard concealed the wheels is clearly visible.

On the opposite wall was a row of windows, and at one end a slow burning coke stove, a larger version of those used in the small mammal and parrot houses. There were doors at each end which were kept open in summer; these enabled visitors to be admitted on a walk through basis. Inside the cage, heavy rings were set into the floor, to which Gert and Daisy could be tethered — this for their own benefit, to protect them from the over enthusiastic attentions of some visitors — and at the rear of the cage were wide doors giving access to an area of orchard at the rear where the animals could roam and relax when off duty. A bear pit was also made; this was a large circular depression lined with concrete and surrounded by a sturdy

Cocky the cockatoo.

wall. Designed to house three Malayan bears, it had a tree in the middle, up which the bears could climb in full view of the public, but completely safely.

In addition, the Children's Corner was greatly enlarged. More enclosures, with paintings on the rear walls by Sir Garrard, were added, and two dolls' houses with glazed fronts were built, one named "Hotel Rat" and the other "Mouse Villa".

Twenty new aviaries and enclosures were also built to house a collection of pheasants, and additional small birds and animals which Sir Garrard acquired. These occupied in all several acres of orchard, which provided an attractive setting in which to view the new arrivals.

Sadly, in January, Sally the elephant suffered an infection of her trunk. At that time, antibiotics had not been heard of, and veterinary surgeons had little experience in dealing with the illnesses of exotic animals. Everything possible in the light of current knowledge was done; but an elephant without a trunk which works cannot live, and less than twelve hours after the onset of her illness, poor Sally died.

By March all the winter work was done and Stanley Holloway came to open the Zoo for the 1939 season. Despite bitterly cold weather, a large crowd attended, and persuaded Holloway to recite one of his monologues, "Albert and the Lion". This tells the story of a small boy who visited a zoo and ignored the good advice he was given, suffering a miserable fate as a result. Afterwards Holloway was presented with a framed painting of a pride of lions done by Mr. Swan, a well known local painter of animals, and Mrs. Holloway with a bouquet of flowers, which had almost certainly been grown by Head Gardener Hussey in the Cobtree greenhouses.

Then Holloway, who was to remain a star for many years — perhaps his most memorable role was as Mr. Doolittle in the film of "My Fair Lady" — led the platform party on a rather hasty tour of the new facilities, including Children's Corner, which was renamed Pets' Corner. With their teeth chattering they also briefly admired some of the animals which had arrived during the winter. These included a Bengal tiger, some Japanese raccoon dogs, a Gujerat zebu (the largest Indian humped cattle), twelve varieties of pheasant, some beautiful plumed starlings and some Chinese blue magpies. It was no doubt with relief that the distinguished guests

One of the Bengal tigers.

Fred Youell showing Enid Basnett the art of harnessing.

finally retreated to the Manor House to take tea with Sir Garrard and Lady Edna.

Until now, only two women had been employed at Cobtree, Joan Corner, who worked in the pay box, and an older lady, Mrs. Carry, who looked after Children's Corner. Following the extension of the Children's Corner and its renaming as Pets' Corner, it was felt that a younger girl was needed there, and Enid Basnett was engaged to start in May; the first of many young women later to work at the Zoo. Apart from George Thorneycroft and "Captain" Gates, the male staff at this time included Reg Yardley, Jack Love, Cyril Brett, Fred Cuddington and Fred Youell, who was stud groom, many of the workers living on the estate. Carl Fischer left to take up a position with Chapman's Circus, and the "Captain" began to look after the elephants. Staff now wore a uniform when visitors were present — a yellow jacket with maroon collar and cuffs, and a peaked cap for the men. Mucking out and other dirty jobs were, as far as possible, completed before 11 o'clock when the gates of the Zoo were opened.

Enid Basnett was not the only newcomer at Pets' Corner: other arrivals included two silver fox cubs, four red fox cubs and a baby badger named Billy. The new dolls' houses proved very popular; visitors were fascinated at the spectacle of the small inmates, some brightly coloured, running from room to room and scampering up and down the stairs as they played. Indeed, it was sometimes difficult to persuade them to move on and see the other new attractions. These included Noah's Ark, which contained separate cages for pairs of ferrets, polecats, rabbits and guinea-pigs, and a fine model railway. An extra charge of 2d. for both children and adults was now made for admission to Pets' Corner but babies in arms continued to be allowed in free.

In May there were some more new arrivals. Three husky dogs which had taken part in the Bird Arctic Expedition of 1937/38 found a sanctuary in Wolf Wood, an un-named almost fully grown male chimpanzee joined the strength, and one of England's most beautiful mammals a half grown otter from nearby East Kent, was brought to the Zoo.

Television at that time was in its infancy, the first public transmissions in the world having been started by the B.B.C. in 1936. The few people who did already own a television set were able, during those last few months of peace, to watch a programme in which Sir Garrard described his Zoo and answered questions about its inmates and how it was run. He was not entirely a stranger to broadcasting — he had previously taken part in three radio programmes, the first in the very earliest days of the B.B.C. — and his showman's instincts served him well in this new medium.

At about the time Sir Garrard was doing well on television, a pair of rhesus monkeys were causing havoc back at the Zoo. One Saturday, they found a weak spot in the roof of their cage, and by working diligently on it succeeded in making a large hole, through which they promptly escaped, setting off without delay for the River Medway. They paused en route at a dairy farm, and then took a breather at the Malta Inn at Allington Lock. Their absence was soon noticed, and Zoo staff set out in hot pursuit; by the time they reached the Malta Inn, however, the monkeys had moved on, and they were not seen again until the following afternoon.

They were finally sighted at Sandling Farm, surrounded by indignant chickens whose food they were calmly eating. A party went out to recover them, and some tempting snacks — bananas, apples and so on — were laid out in a conveniently empty chicken house. For some time, the monkeys remained unimpressed by the bait; finally, however at about 5.30 one succumbed and was safely captured. The other was made of sterner stuff, and it was 9.30 before he too surrendered to the authorities. Meanwhile, the hole in their cage had been repaired, and the roof minutely examined to ensure that no more breakouts could be undertaken.

In July a bevy of film, stage and radio stars, including John Mills, Sebastian Shaw, Robertson Hare, Alfred Drayton, Elizabeth Allan and Christopher Stone, came to Maidstone to take part in a gala concert at the Granada Cinema in aid of the People's Dispensary for Sick Animals. Sir Garrard and Lady Edna invited them all to visit the Zoo in the afternoon prior to the performance. It was intended to be a private occasion, but word got out that the celebrities were coming, and a huge crowd, well equipped with autograph books, was waiting to welcome them. The guests

A polar bear surveying the visitors.

responded well, signing hundreds of books and playing with the animals in front of an appreciative audience.

A few weeks later, a very different visitor came to Cobtree to address the members of the Zoo Club, which Sir Garrard had inaugurated. This was David Seth Smith, Curator of Mammals and Birds at the London Zoo, better known to millions of people as the B.B.C.'s "Zoo Man". After his lecture he toured the Zoo, and was among the first people to see two new arrivals, a young bush baby and Ferdinand, a Dexter bull calf.

It was during the summer of 1939 that Sir Garrard decided to give his Zoo a new name. The title Kent Zoo Park had never really taken on, and in any case, its use meant that every item of publicity produced had to give precise details of the location. The new name which he chose, Maidstone Zoo Park, made the description of its whereabouts simpler, and as well, corresponded with the name which most people actually used.

Shortages and Doodlebugs

THE name change was one of the last changes to take place at Cobtree
before, on 3rd September, Great Britain declared war on Nazi Germany. Immediately, by government order, all places of entertainment,
including zoos, were closed. Following this, posses of officials rapidly
descended on Cobtree to inspect the cages and enclosures; they soon confirmed that "all the cages containing possibly dangerous animals are considered to be of such construction that they cause no problems". The Zoo
possessed no poisonous reptiles, and so it was permitted to re-open after
about ten days.

Entrance charges remained unchanged at 6d. for adults and 4d. for
children — members of the forces in uniform came in free. The prices
were very reasonable considering that it now cost as much as 2/6d. (12½p)
to go greyhound racing at Rochester and 1/- (5p) to visit Allington Castle,
with an extra shilling to see the grounds. Despite the chaos all round, the
rest of the season passed uneventfully until, at the end of October, the
Zoo closed to face the first winter of war.

Despite the uncertainty of the times, Sir Garrard could see no reason
for closing down his Zoo, but he did decide to delay introducing any major
new developments. Instead the winter of the so-called "phoney war" was
spent refurbishing and repainting the already existing facilities at Cobtree.
At the same time he kept his eyes open for any animal bargains which
might come on to the market. There were quite a few of these, for all the
circuses in the country had been closed by government order, and most
of them were anxious to dispose of their animal stocks.

Prices reflected the state of the market: a lion which a few years
previously would have fetched £50 to £100 could now be picked up for as
little as £10. At one sale Sir Garrard purchased Lizzie, a fifteen year old
Indian elephant seven feet six inches high, and her inseparable companion,
a black Shetland mare named Dannie, who had been with Little Tom

Fossett's Circus. The circus had come off the road in Wales, so elephant, pony and keeper made the journey to Kent together on foot — an unlikely combination to meet on the road, and one which would be quite impossible today. Lizzie was a good performer, but she had an obstinate streak in her, of which Sir Garrard was warned; however, he forgot all about it, with consequences a few months later which were not easy to forget.

The Zoo was re-opened on 17th March, 1940, by S. J. Warmington, who played the lead character in a popular radio series called "Inspector Hornleigh Investigates". Although the ceremony was in a much lower key than in previous years, and admission charges had gone up to 1/- (5p) for adults and 6d. (2½p) for children and Forces in uniform, a good crowd attended, and renewed acquaintance with many of the Zoo's favourite inmates. Some losses had taken place during the winter however, among them the only kangaroo the Zoo ever owned, and Martha, the companion of Albert the chimp, her name soon being passed on to another female chimpanzee.

Lizzie after her walk from Wales.
Her keeper is on her back and her friend Dannie stands close by.

A few weeks later, in May, there was a second opening ceremony, this time performed by Catherine Hale-Munro, the five year old daughter of Jessie Matthews and Sonnie Hale. Catherine travelled with her parents on the train from Chatham Road station to the Zoo, Jessie commenting that the engine she had named on her last visit looked in good shape; on arrival Catherine cut a tape and somewhat belatedly declared Pets' Corner open for the season. She was allowed to pick up and cuddle some of the animals, and was presented with a toy elephant before touring the rest of the Zoo with her parents. They were among the first visitors to see Nina, a monkey which had been rescued by the Royal Navy from a German merchant ship sunk in the South Atlantic.

At about this time Lizzie, the elephant which had walked from Wales, revealed the wayward streak about which Sir Garrard had been warned. Normal methods of advertising were becoming difficult: newsprint was rationed, newspapers and magazines were getting smaller. Sir Garrard began to look for other ways to publicise his Zoo, and thought up an original idea. Lizzie would be walked into Maidstone, there to parade along the principal streets, and dramatically draw attention to Cobtree Manor and the attractions it offered.

Initially all went well: Lizzie behaved impeccably, and was seen by thousands of people. On the return journey, however, she decided to assert her independence. At the Running Horse public house she should have turned and taken the road to Allington which led to one of the rear entrances to the Zoo; her keepers expected no difficulties at the junction, for up to then she had been as good as gold. But now when they turned, Lizzie did not. After a few moments of somewhat undignified confusion, the keepers attempted to explain her mistake to her, but Lizzie didn't want to know. They cajoled, they pushed, they prodded and they pulled; it made no difference, Lizzie wanted to go straight on, and in due course straight on she went.

The keepers, if somewhat breathless, were not unduly worried: Lizzie's preferred route, though slightly longer, led to the public entrance to Cobtree Manor, where they could easily take her in. When they arrived at the gate, however, Lizzie again showed no desire to deviate from her chosen path. Home, it seemed, held no attractions for her. There was much argument — then on once more the party went — one contented elephant and two very tired keepers. Finally, long after dark, after a journey round almost the entire perimeter of the Cobtree Manor estate and as far

as Lower Bell, Lizzie was persuaded to go home by way of
another entrance, and was bedded
down at last with her two companions, Gert and Daisy.

Meanwhile, meat rationing
had arrived, which, if it created
some difficulties for the human
population, created considerably
greater ones in satisfying the needs
of large meat-eating animals. The
Zoo had always bought in horses,
ponies and donkeys for slaughter,
and also accepted them as gifts, and
now Sir Garrard intensified his
efforts to secure donations of this
kind. Even so, some tightening of
belts among the lions, tigers and so
on was inevitable. There are no
records to show if this impaired
their good humour or not.

*Sir Garrard on his daily tour of
inspection, which he liked to carry
out every morning.*

The import of wild animals
was of course prohibited as soon as war broke out, but the Zoo's collection
continued to grow by natural means. During the first summer of wartime,
a leopard cub was born, as well as a zebu calf, two spotted fallow deer
and some Soay lambs. In addition, Sir Garrard acquired some monkeys
from sailors who brought them home as pets only to find when they reached
England that there was no one to look after them — more and more wives,
mothers and girlfriends were going out to war work or were being called
up to join the Women's Services; and he was able to buy a fine pair of
American bald-headed eagles.

Another contretemps involving an elephant occurred later in the
summer, although this time the animal was scarcely to blame. The Battle
of Britain was reaching its climax, and one sunny afternoon a fighter plane
flew low overhead while Daisy was giving rides; she took fright and bolted
for the elephant house and safety. Fortunately, the keepers were able to
get the children aboard the howdah off before it hit the top of the elephant
house door, and no one was hurt. But elephant rides were discontinued,

All aboard for an elephant ride. Carl Fischer is leading the elephant.
The block and tackle was for placing and removing the howdah.

although details of the times and prices (3d. adults, 2d. children) continued to appear in the official Programme, which had become noticeably thinner, for several years.

After this, despite the upheavals in the outside world, the battles which took place in the skies above, and the bombs which fell on many of the towns and villages of Kent, life in the Zoo continued relatively uneventfully — although, as was to be expected, the number of visitors showed a marked decline — until the season ended after one of the warmest and sunniest summers of the century.

The warm summer was followed by a long, cold winter; water troughs and water pipes froze, and many of the animals needed extra bedding to protect them from the harsh conditions. During the long hours of blackout, it became impossible to carry on with many jobs, and to add to the difficulties, wartime call-up and the need for men to work in the defence industries began to affect the staff at Cobtree, as it had a quarter of a century earlier, during the First World War. Cyril Brett was among those who were called to the services, Jack Love and Fred Cuddington, who had combined the duties of bear-keeper and slaughterman, left to do essential work elsewhere, and Reg Yardley volunteered as a special constable. Only George Thorneycroft, "Captain" Gates, young Enid Basnett, Fred Youell and one of the older keepers remained with Sir Garrard throughout.

To help keep things going, Mrs. Hussey, wife of the head gardener at the Manor, took over from Joan Corner in the paybox, and to replace the other lost staff, a host of young girls was recruited straight from school; inevitably, however, many would soon themselves be called up to serve in the Women's Land Army or do war work, and fresh replacements from school would have to be sought. In these difficult times, Sir Garrard turned his hand to anything that needed to be done, just as he had when a young man working with Lord John Sanger's Circus.

Everyone, permanent staff and temporary workers alike, were saddened when, little more than twelve months after her epic walk from Wales to Kent, Lizzie, the elephant with a mind of her own, suffered a massive heart attack and died. It was thought that perhaps the long walk had in fact been too much for her; be that as it may, she had proved a good natured, loveable beast despite her obstinate streak, and she was greatly missed.

Like all things, the long, cold winter came at last to an end, and to open the 1941 season, John Mills came from London with the entire cast of the Windmill Theatre show "Revudeville". The presence of so much

OFFICIAL
3d
ILLUSTRATED GUIDE
(7th.EDITION)

Sir Garrard Tyrwhitt-Drake's
ZOO PARK
COBTREE MANOR
MAIDSTONE.

Sir Garrard's cover for the 1940 Zoo Guide.

glamour attracted a large crowd to Cobtree, and the opportunity was taken
to urge all of them to help keep the animals fed by bringing their food
scraps and leavings, no matter how trivial, to the Zoo; potato and carrot
peelings, the outside leaves of cabbages and other green vegetables, stale
crusts and anything else that would not be eaten at home would be welcome,
Sir Garrard said, adding that bins would be placed near the main entrance
in Chatham Road where the offerings could be left. He went on to assure
everyone that the Zoo grew as much of its requirements as it could, including
cabbage, lettuce, root vegetables and sunflower seeds, and it made full use
of natural resources such as groundsel, which was carefully collected;
further, bought in food used in the Zoo was mostly unfit for human
consumption, the only exceptions being corn and a few other items which
were all obtained under licence from the Ministry of Agriculture, which
was anxious that the nation's zoos should be preserved.

John Mills had married only a few weeks prior to the ceremony, and his wife, Mary Hayley Bell, was presented with a bouquet of Head Gardener Hussey's finest carnations as she and her husband arrived at the gate beyond the paybox which led to the Manor House; later, after he had declared the Zoo open for the 1941 season, John Mills himself received an animal statuette in bronze. Then he and Mrs. Mills embarked on the usual tour of the Zoo with the other invited guests, during which they saw a female Bengal tiger which had recently arrived, a new pair of llamas, and a mandrill. Tea at the Manor followed, during which Lady Edna presented silver cigarette cases to Miss A. Singer and Miss M. McGrath in recognition of their bravery during the London blitz; together they had rescued a number of horses trapped in stables which enemy bombs had set ablaze.

Inflation, something to which the nation grew accustomed later in the century, had made its appearance in the land since the war began, and admission prices at Cobtree rose to keep pace with it. Adults now had to pay 1/2d. (6p) for a ticket, and children 7d. (3p); but a day at the Zoo still represented good value for money compared with other entertainments — especially one day in May when the entire company of the Windmill Theatre again deserted London for an afternoon in Kent. The occasion was advertised as a Gala Day but no extra charge was made for admission.

At about the same time as the lovely ladies of the Windmill came to Cobtree, a male visitor from London arrived for a longer stay. He was a young lion cub who had been born at the Regents Park Zoo and was called Spitfire, probably in honour of the fighter plane which played such a prominent part in the Battle of Britain. The name suited him well, for he was a bundle of energy and would chase anything in sight, from a fallen leaf to a fly, for hours on end. Two American ostriches, which he would very likely have regarded as a tasty snack, arrived at about the same time — just too late to admire the cherry blossom, which was exceptionally fine that year.

A little later, in July, a rally to honour the Land Girls employed in Kent was organised at the Zoo. Over 1,000 girls attended, and after listening to some speeches — one hopes not too many and not too long — they toured the grounds, met some of the animals, and were entertained to tea, which must have been a pleasant change from their usual daily chores of milking, weeding and mucking out. It is not clear whether or not they met Dinah Tanner, one of the girls who had started work in March, or if so whether they would have fancied a job with which, together with Gordon Paton,

The enclosures in Pets' Corner.

George Thorneycroft feeding the pelican watched by fascinated children.

another young employee, she had been entrusted. This was the hand rearing of a lion cub whose mother didn't do very well with it. The cub shared its quarters with a small mongrel dog called Jed, with whom it lived in perfect harmony, although at meal times the two were separated in order to ensure that Jed got a fair stab at the eatables.

One night a little later an enemy bomb fell near the small mammal house, scoring a direct hit on an aviary which was normally the home of the Zoo's collection of silky bantams. By great good fortune they had been moved out before the bomb fell, so there were no casualties, but the aviary building completely vanished, leaving only a large crater to mark the spot where it had once stood.

Apart from this incident, the summer of 1941 passed relatively peacefully, and during the following winter it was found possible to introduce a few new features to the Zoo. Pets' Corner was further enlarged, and some small wild animals joined its existing population of farm and domestic beasts. And Rabbit Castle, whose name is self explanatory, was built near the main entrance to the grounds. Sadly, as the time for re-opening approached, Albert the chimp, who had become one of the best loved animals at the Zoo, died.

The turnover of staff continued; many of the girls who came straight from school to Cobtree found the work hard and disagreeable and soon left. Often they found that they had simply jumped out of the frying pan into the fire, for although some were soon directed into war factories, others found themselves drafted into the Land Army, where they often encountered similar duties — mucking out, humping bales of fodder, getting water out of frozen tanks and so on — as they had at Cobtree, but with cows and pigs to deal with instead of exotic animals and birds; Dorothy Reeves, one of the girls who came at this time, enjoyed the work however and stayed for two years, until she too had to move on to a job at West Malling; and another girl who found the work congenial was Joyce Theobald.

Richard Hearne, who was starring in a show at the Princes Theatre, opened the Zoo for the 1942 season; Fay Compton accompanied him, and opened the enlarged Pets' Corner, which was officially renamed the Children's Zoo. The new title never really caught on, however, and most people continued to use the old one. During his speech Sir Garrard again emphasised that none of the food used at the Zoo was suitable for human consumption. Swill bins from the two army barracks in the area were delivered on a regular basis to Cobtree, Sir Garrard's chauffeur did a round of the greengrocers and food shops in the neighbourhood two or three times a week to collect waste and, as in the past, old and unwanted horses and domestic animals were taken for slaughter. In addition, Cobtree continued to grow as much fodder for its own use as possible. Despite all this, however, criticism continued to be expressed from time to time at the Zoo's continued existence.

The season saw a marked reduction in the number of visitors, which was not surprising considering the situation in which the country was placed. Maidstone was in a so-called "restricted area", which meant that travellers from outside needed a permit to enter; vast numbers of men and women were away on active service, those still at home were working long hours, and holidays were something scarcely to be thought of. In an effort to cover his costs, Sir Garrard was reluctantly compelled to raise admission charges to 1/3d. (6½p) for adults and 9d. for children. The price of the

Page three of the 1940 Guide. Strangely the admission prices quoted are not the same as those appearing in advertisements that year.

Official Guide however remained the same — it cost 3d. — although it was much thinner, no longer contained any advertisements, and its cover was made from surplus copies of the 1939 cover on which the words "Sixth Edition" had been blacked out and replaced with "Ninth Edition".

May saw the birth of a baby wallaby, which some of the visitors who did manage a trip to Cobtree were lucky enough to see peeping out of its mother's pouch. And in July the girls of the Land Army were again invited to spend a day at the Zoo, with tea to round things off.

In the same month Dinah Tanner had a day to remember. The lion cub which she and Gordon Paton had reared was now too large to handle, and had been put in a cage with another cub of its own age. During her lunch break Dinah often went to see how the cub was progressing, and would stroke it through the bars of its cage. Usually the cub welcomed her attentions, but one day it suddenly became disagreeable, and snapped at her, biting off the tip of the middle finger of her right hand. Sir Garrard was out at the time, and Dinah was hurried to West Kent General Hospital on a milk lorry for treatment. She was away from work for about three weeks following the accident, and has a short finger on her right hand to remind her of it to this day.

At about the same time Sir Garrard agreed to take into his collection a parrot whose owner was finding it difficult to feed under wartime conditions. The bird was an excellent talker, but unfortunately it must have spent its formative years in bad company, for its language consisted almost exclusively of oaths and obscenities, so much so that there were complaints from visitors. Sir Garrard was compelled to remove it from the Zoo to the private aviary at the Manor House where it is to be hoped that no one was offended.

Despite the war, zoos continued to exchange animals among themselves, and during the year Sir Garrard sent Prince, the Gujerat zebu he had bought in 1939, North to Belle Vue Zoo, which possessed a solitary female named Dolly. Prince soon settled in at his new home, and he and Dolly lived happily together in Manchester for eleven years until Dolly's death in 1953.

The Zoo closed to face another winter of war in October. Only minimal maintenance work could be undertaken because of the growing scarcity of building materials and supplies of all kinds, and extensions were out of the question. Make do and mend was the order of the day, essential safety repairs to the cages housing dangerous animals being the only major activity wartime regulations permitted.

One consequence of this was an unpleasant experience for Enid Basnett. Near the paybox were a few so called "open cages" which housed some monkeys and birds. They were simple structures, with a wooden floor raised a little from ground level to keep vermin out, a roof and three sides made of wire mesh, and an enclosed sleeping area made of wood at the rear. One day as Enid was cleaning out the cages, shutting the inmates as usual into their sleeping quarters while she did so, her foot went through a rotten floorboard, and she suddenly found herself trapped in the cage and quite unable to move. It was a quiet spot at the best of times, leading nowhere but to the paybox, and in winter, there were few people around. Enid's cries for help went unheard for over half an hour; finally, however, it was noticed that she was missing and a search was mounted. She was then soon found and released from her uncomfortable position, grazed, bruised, stiff and cold, but fortunately otherwise unharmed.

By March 1943 the Zoo was ready to face its fourth wartime summer. All that was possible in the circumstances had been done to prepare for the new season; many of the animals had been moved so that interesting new arrivals, born during the winter or previous autumn, could be placed in prominent positions. And the restricted area regulations had been lifted, so Sir Garrard could reasonably hope for better attendances.

Nine hundred people turned up for the opening ceremony, the largest number since the war began, which made an encouraging start. It was performed by Jeanne de Casalis, a star of stage and cinema, and also famous on radio as Mrs. Feather, who was supported by Richard Hearne and his wife, the actress Yvonne Ortner, and Alfred Bossom, the M.P. for Maidstone,

Scientific device for feeding Belinda the lamb. Squibs the cat presumably awaits the drops from the rich man's table.

and his son. Jeanne de Casalis amused the crowd with some comedy in her Mrs. Feather vein, and then, speaking more seriously, spoke of Cobtree's beauty and her regret that despite living only a few miles away at Charing, today's visit was her first. But . . . "I shall come again soon!" she said. Sir Garrard presented her with a mounted eagle owl's feather, telling her as he did so that the owl was reputedly not only the wisest but also the luckiest of all birds; and after the usual conducted tour of the Zoo, the platform party was entertained to a modest tea — in keeping with wartime food rationing — in the Manor.

By Whitsun it was clear that Sir Garrard's hopes of better attendances had been justified, and as a result he reduced the admission charge for adults back to 1/-. For some reason, however, the price for children remained unchanged at 9d.

On Whit Monday afternoon the Band of the Royal West Kent Regiment played a selection of wartime musical favourites to a large crowd, who also had an opportunity to see the Zoo's newest lion cubs, recently born to Alice and Mia. These births were something of an achievement for Cobtree, for although all the animals continued to be well fed, the effects of wartime shortages were beginning to be felt, and many species of wild animal were breeding less prolifically as a result.

This was a source of much regret to Sir Garrard who in the past had undertaken several carefully planned experiments in the breeding of unusual animals. He had, for example, tried unsuccessfully to produce a tigon, by crossing a tiger and a lioness; but now he did succeed in producing an animal very similar to the extinct quagga by mating a Grant's zebra with a domestic ass. The resultant foal, when fully grown, was taller than either of its parents, had a dun coloured head and body with the dorsal cross markings of an ass, faint stripes on its flanks and legs and was known as a zebroid.

To improve his wolf pack, in July Sir Garrard purchased three wolf cubs, and about the same time his aviary welcomed a newcomer whose survival was a miracle and whose past was wrapped in mystery. This was a parrot who was dug out alive after being buried for five days in the bombed ruins of what had been his home, and who was able to tell his rescuers nothing except that his name was Freddie. Nobody at the Zoo knew whether or not his former owner had survived, or indeed from whence he came, since the location of all wartime bombing incidents was a closely guarded secret — "somewhere in the South" covering anywhere

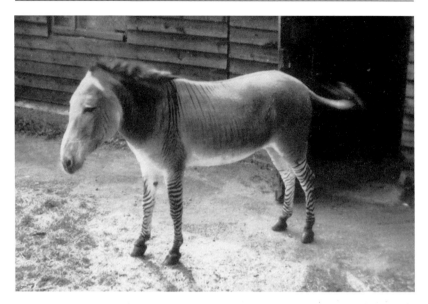

A zebroid, the result of one of Sir Garrard's experiments in cross breeding.

between Bournemouth and Ipswich. Freddie soon recovered from his ordeal and took up residence in the parrot house, where he was always happy to tell visitors his name.

On the August Bank Holiday, then the first Monday in the month, the Band of the Royal West Kent Regiment again entertained visitors to Cobtree; but for much of the time the Zoo was a quiet place that summer. Sometimes there was a commotion in the neighbourhood of the large open fish tank which housed the frogs and toads; when feeling particularly lively, some of these beasts would take it into their heads to jump out, and it then became Dinah Tanner's job to round up the slippery runaways and return them to their home. It was quite a task, for they tended to head for the orchards and paddocks, and some no doubt, escaped Dinah's grasp and found themselves new homes by the river not far away. The penguins Pip and Squeak also quite often caused a diversion, for they loved to wander round the Zoo, to the special delight of children, who would try to hand feed them, and sometimes to catch them — invariably in both cases without success.

At the end of October the Zoo closed, and a quiet summer was followed by a quiet winter, although one incident was probably not considered quiet by "Captain" Gates and was almost his undoing. On one evening he was in more hurry than usual to get a yak settled into its sleeping quarters. He was, perhaps, more enthusiastic in his persuasion than he should have been and the animal took exception and charged him.

Enid relates "I was working some distance away when I heard a yell; I turned to see "Captain" Gates flying through the air, arms and legs in all directions, like a rag doll. I rushed to the scene, fearful of what I might find, but discovered him picking himself up, outside the compound, with nothing worse than a bruised body and battered pride. The yak had tossed him right over the compound fence." Enid continues, "It was probably fortunate that it did, for if he had fallen inside the fence and the animal had continued its attack, the result could have been very serious indeed."

Life was hard for the staff, who like the animals — and everyone else in the country — were affected by food rationing and the growing shortages of goods and services of all kinds. Sir Garrard had extra responsibilities

Jacob's sheep en route to fresh pastures. On the left is the cattle house, in the far distance the aquarium and on the right the parrot house.

to cope with, for in August he had again been elected Mayor of Maidstone, and war conditions added greatly to the duties of that office.

Nevertheless, spring came at last, and with it, despite the difficulties, a new crop of animal births to make the struggles of the previous months seem worthwhile. There were one or two Royal Cream foals, some lion cubs, and as usual, many baby rabbits, guinea pigs and other small animals.

The Zoo re-opened for the 1944 season in March; in his introductory speech, Sir Garrard felt constrained to refer once again to criticisms about the provision of food for animals at a time when the human population was going short. The food the animals eat was simply unfit for human consumption, he said, adding that the carnivores were often getting meat which would normally be regarded as unfit even for them. Apart from this, food waste and swill formed the major part of the other animal's diets, with a very small corn allowance which was granted by the Ministry of Food precisely because it saw the Zoo as a vital contribution to the war effort. It offered tired workers the chance of a day's relaxation in peaceful surroundings, he went on, it paid entertainment tax on every penny received in admission charges, and then it paid the government 75% of whatever profit it finally made.

Sir Garrard then introduced the stage and radio star Mabel Constanduras, who was accompanied by the Zoo's old friend, Richard Hearne. After she had declared the Zoo open, Sir Garrard presented her with a statuette depicting two lions in combat, and the usual tour of the Zoo then followed. Before the visitors retired to the Manor for a wartime tea with Sir Garrard and Lady Edna they were able to see for themselves that despite all the shortages and difficulties, the Zoo's animal collection remained as large as ever, and that the animals were being maintained to the highest standards of health and well-being.

Admission charges remained unchanged at 1/- for adults and 9d. for children; it is not known if prices at the café were also unaltered. The café at Cobtree suffered from shortages as much as every other institution in the land; nevertheless, visitors could still get a cup of tea there which was hot if not very strong, and meals and snacks of a sort continued to be provided. F. A. Smith & Son Ltd. had taken over responsibility for the catering from Mr. Beslee, and during the war years Victoria Paul was the Manageress; she worked wonders in maintaining a service throughout hostilities.

The Official Guide for 1944 was not only even thinner than the previous edition, partly because the cover was printed on similar paper to the contents and partly because of the lack of advertisements, but also smaller, the page size being reduced to 5″ × 3⅞″ from 7¼″ × 5¾″. Inside was a message from Sir Garrard headed "An Apology and an Explanation", which read "I regret that owing to the shortage of labour, particularly male, the impossibility of obtaining materials of all sorts for repairs and renovation, and the lack of white sawdust for the cages, this Zoo cannot be kept as clean and neat as it is under normal conditions. Still, after 4½ years of war it is something to have it stocked and kept as it is!". Normally he produced an animal drawing for the cover; this year, for the first and probably the only time, a photograph was used. The block was almost certainly pre-war, for the picture was of four lion cubs born in August 1937 sitting together in a basket, and had appeared previously in the contents pages. The price remained 3d. (and was still unchanged in 1954, the last edition of which a copy has been found).

Soon after the summer season had started, Enid and Dinah were returning one morning from a trip to the dung heap, which was located near the slaughterhouse behind the bear cages, in an enclosure not open to the public, when the Cobtree camel managed somehow to escape from his enclosure. He saw the two girls, and at once made a bee-line for them: camels are strong and at times forceful beasts, and Enid and Dinah, seeing what was approaching, stood not upon the order of their going, but abandoning their wheelbarrow, went — full pelt for the nearest refuge, which was the parrot house. They reached it safely, but the camel attempted to follow them in, not considering however, that his hump was higher than his head. He got stuck fast in the doorway, enabling Enid and Dinah to leave the parrot house from the other end and seek help from George Thorneycroft. When the three of them returned the wretched animal was still stuck, head in the parrot house and behind outside, but the disappearance of the girls appeared to have quietened him somewhat. With a lot of pushing and pulling he was finally released and consented to be led back to his enclosure, fortunately none the worse for his escapade.

The experience underlined the wisdom of designing most of the Zoo's houses on a walk-through basis; for one thing it enabled the girls to escape, and for another it was almost certainly their disappearance which calmed the camel down. The damage he might have done to himself, the parrot house, the parrots and not least to Enid and Dinah, if they had remained in view and he had continued to struggle to free himself, are best left to the imagination. What no one can explain, however, is why he appeared to take such a dislike to them that day, or how he got out of his enclosure.

Throughout the war, the girls who stood in for the absent men at Cobtree undertook almost all the duties of caring for the non-ferocious beasts and small animals at the Zoo, as well as the sheep and goats, Sir Garrard's Royal Cream ponies, and all the birds. They also supervised the pony rides, which remained as popular as ever, and which were in greater demand in 1944 than they had been the previous year; for despite the absence of so many people from their homes, and the heavy calls made on those remaining — queuing for their rations, firewatching, digging for victory, knitting for the troops or fund-raising to buy comforts for them — the attendance figures at Cobtree were up. The opportunity of a few hours away from it all, and the chance to see some living things unaffected by the war, seemed to act as a magnet to the people of mid Kent. They came in their hundreds, to laugh at the antics of the monkeys and the chimpanzees, to watch the elephants display their circus tricks — a popular act had them sucking dust off the ground in order to blow it at the audience — and then, perhaps, to walk awhile in the orchards or through the quiet woods and shed some of the tensions and anxieties of daily life.

Two births were recorded at the Zoo in September which would have been remarkable at any time, but which were doubly so in war conditions.

Cages for the big cats.

The first, and also a first for the Zoo, was a baby peccary, or South American wild pig, and the second, a baby capatrix, or West African monkey. This was an even greater success for Sir Garrard, for like many monkeys, the capatrix very rarely breeds in captivity. The little newcomer caused a few problems however, for the monkey's natural diet includes a lot of fruit, which in general was difficult to obtain in 1944, and in particular bananas, which could not be obtained at all. Somehow or other, nonetheless, the baby and its mother were kept going, and many people came to see them in the few weeks of the season that remained until the Zoo closed once more at the end of October.

On the night of 13th June, 1944, a doodle-bug (a pilot-less jet-engined bomb), the first of Hitler's much heralded secret weapons, fell on East London. From then until the last came down on 29th March, 1945, thousands fell all over the South East of England, causing many deaths and great destruction, but failing entirely to break the morale of the civilian population.

One landed at Cobtree, probably in August or September; the exact date is unknown, since the timing and location of bomb incidents remained an official secret. It exploded in one of the trees by the lake, felling the tree, blowing all the tiles off the roof of the gate house on Chatham Road, which was the home of "Captain" Gates, and breaking all the windows, but fortunately injuring nobody. The Royal Cream ponies often grazed in a field adjoining the lake, but they were elsewhere that night, and the only casualty was an unlucky gnu some distance away who was killed by a random piece of flying metal.

Sir Garrard quickly responded to the incident by hanging a jagged piece of the doodle-bug's casing on the wall of the elephant house facing the cage bearing a message which read approximately: "This is a piece of the b..... doodle-bug sent over by that horrid little man Mr. Hitler to try to blow up our house". The exact wording unfortunately is not known, for it was not recorded at the time, and the doodle-bug casing has been lost.

If the night the doodle-bug fell was particularly memorable for "Captain" Gates, the morning of 3rd November was equally so for Enid Basnett. During the cold weather, many of the animals, including the monkeys, which spent the summer months in the open air, were brought indoors, and some of them were caged in pairs to encourage breeding. One of Enid's winter jobs was to feed and water the inmates of the mammal house; every morning she would walk along the footway between the bars of the cages and the safety barrier, opening the access door of each cage in turn and placing inside a dish of already prepared food. She would replenish each animal's drinking water from outside the cage at the same time, using a water-can with a long spout.

On 3rd November, matters followed their usual course until Enid reached the cage occupied by a monkey named Louis, a pig-tailed macaque, who had spent previous winters in the parrot house; perhaps he didn't like his new surroundings, or perhaps he was disturbed by the presence of females nearby. He had never before given any trouble, but today, as Enid opened the access door to his cage, he made a dive for it, successfully avoided the broom which she always carried with her and streaked out.

Enid had known Louis for several years and was not unduly alarmed; he remained inside the safety barrier, and she thought she could handle him alone. There was a brisk struggle, and finally she managed to capture him and return him to his cage. He was not best pleased at this, however, and vented his spleen by biting her hands as hard as he could. She made him secure, and then set out to seek help, with blood pouring from her injuries. It was a long trek to the Manor House, and on the way she met only one person, a young girl new to the Zoo; so as not to frighten her, instead of asking her for assistance, she hid her hands until they had passed.

Sir Garrard was at home and drove Enid at once to West Kent General Hospital, where it was found that the wounds to her right hand were not too severe, but that Louis had seriously damaged the tendons and leaders of her left hand. The injuries were dressed and Enid was sent home, but by the evening she was in such pain that her father took her back to the hospital. This time she was admitted as an in-patient, and she remained in hospital for five weeks, with many more weeks' out-patient treatment to follow before finally she was able to return to work. Sadly, it proved impossible fully to correct the damage done to her left hand, and she was left permanently with a slight disability. Sir Garrard always maintained that apes and monkeys were unpredictable beasts; and Enid never cared for them again.

In March the Zoo re-opened for the 1945 season, and a record wartime crowd of more than 2,000 turned up for the opening ceremony. The platform party again included Richard Hearne and his wife, Yvonne Ortner, and in addition, their two year old daughter Cetra, to whom Sir Garrard and Lady Edna were godparents, Australian film star Sarah Gregory, and comedian Fred Emney. It was Fred who formally declared the Zoo open. In his speech afterwards he reminded the audience that Cobtree housed the largest privately owned Zoo in Europe, and recorded that over 1½ million

Some of the staff in 1946.
Left to right, Nellie Durling, Enid Basnett, Joyce Theobald and Jean Burles.

people had visited it since 1934; he ended by congratulating Sir Garrard and his staff on the high standards of animal care they had sustained despite all the difficulties caused by the war.

After the speeches, the usual tour of the Zoo took place; Cetra Hearne cut a tape to open Pets' Corner, and was delighted with the cuddly animals she found inside, and the stars signed countless autographs. For the celebrities, a wartime tea in the Manor with Sir Garrard and Lady Edna concluded the proceedings.

Soon after the season started, serious difficulties were encountered in feeding the carnivores. There were no more old horses to be found, and no more pets whose owners were glad to have humanely put down; Sir Garrard was compelled for the only time in his life, to slaughter healthy beasts. Two Royal Cream ponies were sacrificed to keep the irreplaceable collection of lions, tigers and other meat eaters alive. It was a hard decision, but biologically the correct one: there was a large herd of ponies on the estate, they bred well, and the loss could soon be made good. To replace the other beasts after the war would have been difficult even if possible, it would probably have meant depleting the rapidly diminishing wild stocks in the world, and the cost would have been enormous.

The ponies saved the day; most of the staff at Cobtree believed that but for them, most if not all of the Zoo's carnivores would have had to be put down. As it was, the war in Europe ended on 7th May, though hostilities continued in the Far East for three more months, until Hiroshima and Nagasaki ushered in the nuclear age, and food supplies for the animals gradually became easier.

There were quite a lot of births in the Zoo during the last weeks of the war; the coypus, or giant South American water rats had a litter, some lion cubs and two baby wallabies were born, and in Pets' Corner there were numbers of lambs, kids and baby rabbits to cuddle. By July, the first faltering steps in the return to normal life were being taken, although supplies of all kinds remained scarce, and zoos did not rate high in the priority ratings. So the repainting and renovation which Cobtree so urgently needed had still to wait.

A great load had been lifted off peoples shoulders however; they could go out without the fear of finding their homes destroyed in their absence, men and women were beginning to return from service in the forces and factories, and travel was becoming a little easier. More and more people began to visit the Zoo, to see the animals and enjoy the calm and beauty of the woods. Many of them brought food for the animals from their own limited stocks, for food was still rationed and continued to be for many years; and people were not worried at the shabby paintwork or patched up buildings.

In September Elsie and Doris Waters came back to attend a birthday party for Gert and Daisy, the elephants they had christened in 1936, who were now fifteen years old. As a birthday party it was ill-timed, for both the elephants were born in January, but Sir Garrard never lost his show-man's flair, and he knew that the event would bring extra crowds to the Zoo. A birthday cake was made of meal, bran and currants covered in chocolate which was unfit for human consumption, and cut by Elsie and Doris in front of an audience of no less than 5,000 people. After they had given both the elephants a slice of cake, Elsie told the crowd that she and Doris would shortly be going to Rangoon to entertain the British forces still in the Far East, and that they had promised to take a message from the elephants to their relatives in Burma.

A comfortable chimp.

A cream pony waiting for a customer at the pony track.
In the background the pens for the foxes, badgers and coyotes.

Before they left the platform, Sir Garrard presented the two ladies with two wooden carvings depicting the globe held aloft by four elephants with a fifth elephant standing astride above it, after which they mingled with the crowd and signed postcards of Gert and Daisy which were on sale in aid of the Mayoress of Maidstone's fund for the widows and families of servicemen killed in the war. Ten pounds was raised for the fund, which may not seem much, but which represented a lot of signatures if one considers that the normal selling price of the postcards was only 2d. or 3d. Elsie and Doris had certainly earned their tea by the time they finally retired to the Manor.

A few weeks later, after more than 100,000 people had visited the Zoo during the season, it closed for another winter. Finding food for the animals continued to be a problem, but staff difficulties began to ease, and before the Spring Sir Garrard was able to restore the establishment to its pre-war level of about six men and six women. The continuing shortage of building materials limited the amount of refurbishment and new work which could be carried out, but there was one interesting development.

A man named Pentland Hick, who was a director of a firm called Insect Supply Company, and worked in partnership with another business known as Whatkins and Doncaster Natural History, rented an overgrown orchard from Sir Garrard and erected a large ex-army hut on it in which to house an exhibition of butterflies and stick insects. Known as Butterfly Farm, it was not strictly part of the Zoo, and when it opened an extra charge of 3d. was made for admission. It occupied an ideal setting for its purpose, being surrounded by old apple trees; these were used for breeding, various kinds of caterpillars being placed on the branches, which were sleeved to prevent the caterpillars from escaping and the birds from eating them. The collection was not conceived simply as an attraction for the public, but was also intended to provide butterflies, moths and other insects for medical and veterinary research at scientific institutions, universities and schools throughout the country.

Peter Abery went straight from school to work at Butterfly Farm; he enjoyed his two years there and reckons that it gave him a good start in life. He has many memories of it, one of the most vivid being of the day one of the apes escaped from the Zoo and somehow managed to get into it. Peter arrived for work to find the ape surrounded by a collection of very large caterpillars, which he was eating rather quickly and with evident relish. Peter hurried away to seek help; when he returned with several

keepers they found that the ape, who presumably had had enough caterpillars, had gone outside and climbed up a tree, in which he was now
comfortably seated.

Nothing would persuade him to come down; food was tried, but he
was still full of caterpillars and was not interested. Sticks and nets proved
useless, for he was out of reach, and after more than an hour the position
seemed to be one of stalemate. Then, quite suddenly and for no apparent
reason, he decided that he'd been sitting down long enough, and set out
on a wild romp through the orchard, jumping from tree to tree and branch
to branch as he would have done in the wild, pursued by an increasingly
breathless party of keepers. The chase seemed likely to go on indefinitely
when, as suddenly as he had started it, he seemed to grow tired of it. He
turned in the direction of the Zoo, and quite unprompted, ambled back
to his cage, quietly climbed in, and settled down as though nothing out
of the ordinary had happened. No one ever found out how he escaped in
the first place.

Peter never thought that Butterfly Farm had a secure future. It was
not arranged in such an attractive way as later versions, and the majority
of people were not very interested in the breeding habits of caterpillars
and insects, nor was there a great demand for the display cases of mounted
butterflies which were on sale, and on which high hopes had been placed.
He left for East Malling Research Station, and later Shell Research at
Woodstock near Sittingbourne, and was not surprised, about twelve months
after his departure, to hear that it had closed.

Pentland Hick was by nature an entrepreneur and by profession an
entomologist. He went on to become a writer of books and television
scripts, and to own several cinemas in the Scarborough area. Later he was
a pioneer of European dolphinaria and in 1961 he opened Flamingo Park
in Yorkshire, which became one of the most popular open air attractions
in the North of England.

A Royal Visit

ONE day towards the end of March, 1946 a crowd of some 1,500 people assembled at Cobtree for the opening of the Zoo's first postwar season. The ceremony was due to start at 3.15 and Claude Hulbert, who was to officiate, arrived in good time, accompanied by his wife, Enid Trevor and their young daughter Jacqueline. They went first to the Manor, where Sir Garrard and Lady Edna welcomed them, and from whence Sir Garrard led them to the Zoo and the dais which had been set up for the occasion. En route Jacqueline broke away unnoticed, and only when they reached the platform did Claude and his wife realise that their daughter was missing. Proceedings were held up for a while as a search was mounted for her; fortunately she was almost the only person in the Zoo not assembled for the opening ceremony, and she was quite quickly found admiring Gert and Daisy. As soon as she had been re-united with her parents Claude declared the Zoo open, after which he and his wife, keeping a tight hold on Jacqueline, were taken round the Zoo with the other invited guests.

When they reached Pets' Corner, Jacqueline cut a ribbon to open it, which may not have been strictly necessary, as the Zoo had already been opened; but Sir Garrard was a shrewd operator, and the additional ceremony encouraged people to pay the extra 3d. to go in. The animals in fact generally took second place on Opening Day; only those who arrived early took time to see them, the majority of folk being more interested in seeing the celebrities and collecting their autographs. This didn't worry Sir Garrard however, for he knew that most would make a return visit later in the season.

The Butterfly Farm was of course included in the visitors' tour, and they also met Ronald White, who like Pentland Hick had seen an opportunity to develop a new service for patrons of the Zoo. Unlike Hick's idea, however, White's proved an unqualified success. He was a photographer and rented a paddock from Sir Garrard, in which was placed a mural (done by Sir Garrard) featuring a blue sky and a profusion of pink and white blossoms. For a moderate fee parents could have their children photographed astride one of the Royal Cream ponies in front of the mural, with themselves standing alongside if they wished. Only the most docile beasts were employed as mounts; they had names like Duchess, Floppy and Vicky, and sometimes on warm days they almost fell asleep on the job. The service proved immensely popular, and there must indeed be many homes in and around Maidstone which to this day have hidden in a cupboard or drawer a picture of mum or dad on one of the Royal Cream ponies at Cobtree.

A few weeks after opening day, the Zoo welcomed another distinguished visitor, the Rt. Hon. Chuter Ede, M.P., Home Secretary. He requested the invitation, and came to lunch at Cobtree accompanied by the Mayor and Mayoress of Maidstone, Alderman and Mrs. Day, the local M.P., Alfred Bossom, Mr. W. Platts, Clerk to the Kent County Council, and other friends and colleagues, before being taken on a conducted tour of the Zoo. He fed some of the animals and appeared thoroughly to enjoy his day away from affairs of state.

Juney, the Royal Cream pony, on duty in Ronald White's photographic enclosure. Sir Garrard painted the backdrop, the rider is the author of this book.

Although the war was over, Smiths, who still had the catering contract, seem to have found feeding the human visitors to the Zoo still difficult; not only did food rationing remain in force, but catering staff were still hard to find. They were advertising for staff in July and offering good wages; and they were still advertising a month later. The café and snack bar remained open, however, and if service was a little slow, probably no one noticed — after all, service at that time was slow everywhere.

Sir Garrard, on the other hand, was finding recruitment for the Zoo becoming steadily easier. Two young women he engaged in 1946 were Myrtle Rand, for the parrot house, and Nellie Durling, whose duties were mainly to assist in Pets' Corner. Nellie remained at Cobtree for three years and recalls happy days there, apart perhaps from one, when a squirrel, out of sorts for some reason, bit her wrist and refused to let go until she gave him a tap with the brush she used for cleaning out his cage.

Obtaining new animals was also once more possible, import restrictions having been lifted, and in August a family of viscachas arrived from South America. A little later Sir Garrard purchased some blue and yellow macaws, some owls and a pair of night herons. These are blue-black above and white below, with two long white plumes on the nap; their habitat is mostly wooded swampland, and they hunt fish, mainly at night. It is believed that the Zoo's specimens were housed in an enclosure with a pond in it opposite the bisons and quite near to the Manor.

In September a great gale hit Cobtree, and during the night an elm tree was blown down, opening a gap in the fencing around the wallabies' enclosure. Joey, a three year old Australian wallaby, quickly realised that here was an unexpected chance to see something of the Old Country, and he set out without delay through the gap, heading in the general direction of Rochester. He managed to cover eight miles without mishap, although the gale had caused much damage in the area, bringing down several high voltage power lines, and eventually appeared in the village of Borstal, where the village children were amazed to see him. They managed to coax him into the garden of a house in Hill Road, and then to hole him up behind the chicken run. Philip Butterworth from Rochester, who was fourteen, then managed to grab Joey's tail, and to bundle him into the air raid shelter which was still in the garden; and there he remained, his tour over, until the Zoo's van arrived, complete with cage, to take him home. A free day at the Zoo with his family was Philip's reward; no doubt he was interested to meet Joey again, but whether Joey was pleased to see him is not known.

Lined up for a Royal inspection.

Left to right: Myrtle Rand, Jean Burles, "Captain" Gates, Pauline Wilmshurst, Fred Youell, Joyce Theobald, George Thorneycroft, Nellie Durling, Betty Cheyney and Enid Basnett on the day Princess Elizabeth visited Cobtree.

The Royal Party at Sheep Rock.

As usual, towards the end of October the Zoo closed for the winter. This never meant that life for the staff became easier, for winter always brought new tasks, and many of the animals needed more care and attention when the weather was cold than they did in summer. This autumn, however, there was a special urgency in the air and more than usual to do in the way of cleaning and tidying. Materials were still scarce, but much can be done with a nail or two here, a touch of paint or a re-written sign there, and the liberal application of soap and water everywhere. The reason for the urgency was the planned visit next month of a Very Important Person; and by dint of much hard work, by the set date everything was ready.

On the morning of Tuesday, 12th November, Princess Elizabeth, now Her Majesty The Queen, arrived at Cobtree by car, accompanied by her Lady in Waiting, the Hon. Mrs. Elphinstone, and was received by Sir Garrard and Lady Edna. Their other guests, Canon A. O. Standen, the Vicar of Maidstone, and Major J. F. Ferguson, the Chief Constable of Kent, were presented to the Princess, who remained for lunch in the Manor House.

Afterwards, she was conducted through the gardens of the Manor to a private gate which opened on to an open space within the Zoo; the stables were on one side and the granary on the other. The area was open to the public, but largely used to take in deliveries of grain, etc., and to turn tractors and carts. Today the staff was lined up there to be presented to the Princess, who had a few words for everyone. Among those presented was Ronald White; she was told that he had been on active service from 1939 to 1945, and that now, in addition to providing a service to the public at the Zoo, he was Sir Garrard's personal photographer. The Princess gave permission for White to make a photographic record of her visit, and when, after admiring some of

Princess Elizabeth leaving the small mammal house.

In Wolf Wood. There do not seem to be many leaves on the path!

The Princess with Sir Garrard watching the lions being fed.

the Royal Cream ponies which had been turned out for her to inspect, she moved on to tour the Zoo, he followed with his camera at a discreet distance.

The staff meanwhile had dispersed, and most of them sought vantage points from which to watch the Royal progress; Sir Garrard had been on tenterhooks for a week, and they had all worked hard until the last minute to ensure that every path was swept and every cage clean, the latter a specially difficult task, for animals ignore even the most heartfelt requests not to make a mess. Tidying the woods had not been in their remit, however, for Sir Garrard had realised that in autumn, with the leaves falling fast, the task would be impossible; he decided for this reason not to include them in the Princess's tour. He carried with him a chip basket of assorted titbits so that the Princess could watch him feeding and talking to his animals, or feed some of them herself if she wished, and all went well until they left the mammal house. Then she saw a sign pointing to Wolf Wood, and turning to Sir Garrard asked him if indeed there were wolves at Cobtree. On learning that there were, she asked to see them, and so he was compelled, no doubt very reluctantly, to conduct her into the untidied woods. Let us hope that she found the wolves so interesting that she did not notice the unswept leaves.

The visit was a private one, with no press coverage, and preceded an official visit to the Carriage Museum in Mill Street, Maidstone, which Sir Garrard had recently set up, and which the Princess formally opened. It took place just in time, for a few weeks later, what was probably the hardest and coldest winter of the century set in.

Heavy snowfalls were followed by weeks in which the temperature never rose above zero; coal stocks, potato clamps, everything in the land was frozen solid; for two days all the local bus services were withdrawn, and Nellie Durling and her friend Pauline Wilmshurst, who lived in Chatham, walked together both days all the way to Cobtree and back so as not to let down Sir Garrard or the animals.

The lake was of course frozen, but sadly not quite hard enough to bear the weight of one of the Royal Cream ponies which unwarily walked on to it one day. As it approched the centre, the ice gave way beneath it, and the wretched beast fell through. The water was deep, and there was no way in which it could be rescued; indeed, it was many weeks before the body could be recovered. All things come to an end, however, even hard winters, and at last spring approached and with it the time for another Opening Day.

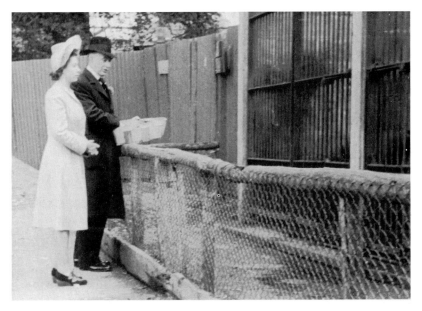

Sir Garrard, complete with basket of goodies for the animals, describes the inmates of the bear cage to the Princess.

Jack Train, famous as Colonel Chinstrap in the popular radio show "Itma", opened the Zoo for the 1947 season. His wife accompanied him, and also on the platform were Olaf Olson who played in the "Paul Temple" adventures, Collie Knox, a leading radio critic, and the Mayor of Maidstone, Cllr. S. J. Lyle. After the speeches, Jack Train was presented with a bottle of champagne, and his wife with a basket of Cobtree new laid eggs — at that time of continued food rationing perhaps more welcome than the champagne. During the tour which, as usual, followed, Jack had a ride on one of the Cream ponies, which delighted the crowds, before retiring to the Manor for the customary tea.

The season turned out to be a quiet one: both the Zoo and its customers needed time to recover from the effects of the previous winter. But in August, always a popular time for introducing new animals — it gave those from warmer climes a chance to adjust to English conditions in easy stages — a fine lioness arrived to improve the breeding stock, and was soon joined, although at a suitable distance, by a Patagonian hare and by some

Jack Train demonstrating his equestrian skill on one of the Royal Cream ponies.

monkeys and fox cubs. A maribou stork from Africa was also purchased, as well as a pair of ravens and a jackdaw. The Cobtree population was further increased by births among the existing inmates; these included a litter of wild pigs and a Gujerat zebu calf, while there was something approaching a population explosion at the Butterfly Farm.

Flossie Rayfield was among the new staff who joined the Zoo at this time. Her main responsibility was the care of the owls: she released those in Pets' Corner each evening so that they could spend the night in their natural habitat, and invariably found them all waiting to be returned to their cages when she arrived at the Zoo next morning. The only duty she did not enjoy was catching and killing mice for them, from the teeming population of Mouse Corner. This was more humane, however, than feeding the birds live mice, some of which might have escaped to add to the Zoo's hygiene problems — and in any case, owls, like everyone else, must live.

After the Zoo had closed for another winter, Sir Garrard was approached by Captain Raynor, a gentleman with a problem — a problem named Tim o'Timilee, an agreeable but rapidly growing leopard. The captain and his wife had found Tim abandoned while on a hunting trip in India, and had rescued and hand reared him, then brought him home with them; but he began to outgrow the facilities of their garden, and to be something of a handful in the house as well. They wondered if Cobtree would take him off their hands. Sir Garrard was not in the market for a leopard at the time, but finally agreement was reached that Cobtree would look after Tim if the Raynors would pay for his food, and for a special cage to be built for him. While this was being erected, Sir Garrard was busy supervising the establishment of a new attraction, a silver fox farm in the Cobtree woods. From a circus, he also bought a young polar bear, one of a performing troupe who didn't prove a very good performer. He quickly took to Zoo life, and settled down very comfortably in his new home.

At this time, Maidstone Corporation was modernising its trolley bus fleet, replacing six-wheelers with four-wheelers, and Sir Garrard purchased two of the redundant six-wheelers. One was placed beside the café, part of it being used as the women's staff room, and the remainder for the preparation of animal food; the other was located near Reg Yardley's cottage and provided temporary accommodation for new staff from outside the district while they found permanent homes. They were regarded as eyesores by some people, but if they had survived until today, would be cherished as almost priceless relics of another age.

On opening day in 1948, the Zoo's fifteenth season, visitors were greeted with a surprise; during the winter a brown bear had given birth to two cubs, Maidstone's first. The news had been kept secret, in case they did not survive, but survive they did, and a few lucky people were able to catch a glimpse of them with their mother. In addition, the silver fox farm was finished, and Tim was installed in his purpose built cage not far from Goat Mountain, all unaware that he was going to add not a little to the difficulties of the Cobtree staff.

Under the terms of their agreement, the Raynors could visit Tim whenever they wished, and they often sat in deckchairs set in the space between the safety barrier and the bars of his cage, watching him, talking to him, and sometimes feeding him. Despite warning notices, visitors seeing this thought they could do the same, and when staff came to remove them there were frequent arguments along the lines of "one law for Them and another law for Us".

Almost-local comedian Eric Barker, who lived at Ashford, and starred in the B.B.C. radio show "Merry-go-Round", opened the new season; his wife, Pearl Hackney, was with him and so once again were Richard Hearne and Yvonne Ortner, as well as Alfred Bossom, M.P., and the Mayor and Mayoress of Maidstone, Cllr. and Mrs. William Day, Jnr. In his speech, Barker spoke of his admiration for Sir Garrard in maintaining his Zoo throughout the war and the hard years since — like the Windmill Theatre, he said, it never closed. He was presented with a bronze of two foxes, while Pearl Hackney was given an emu's egg. The platform party then moved to Pets' Corner, where five year old Petronella Barker cut a ribbon to open it. She had a day to remember, being allowed to stroke and cuddle many of the inmates while her father recorded the scenes with his camera, and then having a ride on the railway before following the grown-ups to the Manor for tea.

A cheerful lad named Sam Carter, liked by everyone, was now the usual engine driver; he remained at Cobtree for several years, and when not engaged on the footplate, acted as assistant to Head Keeper Thorney-croft. A secondhand diesel locomotive had been acquired from a local

George Thorneycroft presenting a bouquet to Pearl Hackney at the private entrance from Cobtree Manor to the Zoo. Behind Sir Garrard is Richard Hearne and in the background is Pearl Hackney's husband, Eric Barker.

Gert at home in the Elephant House.

quarry at some time since the end of the war to replace the steam-outline "Jessie", who presumably had worn out. Avery's did not maintain the replacement engine, the contract for this being awarded to E. A. Gardener & Son of Maidstone. "Jessie" however continued to appear in photographs of the railway in the programme and elsewhere until closure; Sir Garrard never believed in wasting money!

On the other hand, he had a keen eye for a bargain. When Rediffusion wanted a piece of his land on which to erect a radio mast, he included a proviso in the agreement that they should install loudspeakers in the Zoo and provide recorded music free of charge while it was open. One speaker was erected over the café and two or three others in strategic locations elsewhere. Enid Basnett remembers particularly hearing the song "South of the Border, Down Mexico Way" countless times during the years after the war.

The railway suffered its first accident in April: both the coaches came off the lines one day, and two land girls, Miss B. Cawley and Miss V. O'Shea, suffered slight leg injuries. After treatment at West Kent General Hospital they were able to return to their hostel at Wateringbury; no one else was hurt, but the railway was closed for several weeks while the cause of the accident was sought. Possibly the rails, which were not very heavily ballasted, had spread, or perhaps there was an obstruction on the line; we shall never know, for no report was ever published.

Some time before this, Jack Kaye joined the staff. He came from Chapman's Circus, and had a cottage on the estate. A good all-round keeper, he looked after the bears and monkeys, ultimately leaving for a post at Dudley Zoo. In May, a young girl named Thelma Cornelius was recruited. She became responsible for the care of the hoofed animals, and also looked after the emus and rhea, which can be dangerous birds and need careful handling.

Early in her career she made a mistake which earned her a brisk telling off from "Captain" Gates: elephants need a lot of water, and he had a hose pipe leading to their troughs attached to a tap near the parrot house, which he often left trickling, so that while he was busy elsewhere the troughs never emptied. One day Thelma removed the hose to fill some buckets and then forgot to reconnect it. When the good "Captain" returned to his charges to find their troughs empty he was not best pleased. Thelma never made the same mistake again, and went on to become one of the Zoo's most valued keepers, remaining at Cobtree until its final closure. In the same month that she joined the Zoo, a pair of vultures from the Falkland Islands nested, and the female laid two eggs. Unfortunately, there is no record of whether or not they were successfully hatched.

A few weeks later, at the beginning of June, admission fees for adults were increased by a substantial 50%, from 1/- to 1/6d. (7½p), but prices for children remained unchanged, at 9d. Attendance does not seem to have been adversely affected, the steadily growing brown bear cubs proving a great attraction. By July they could be seen, sleeping, boxing with each other, or playing like kittens, almost all day every day. They were known to the staff as our Teddy Bears. Other attractions included seven new

"Would you mind looking after the kids?" Joyce Theobald on baby sitting duty.

One of Thelma Cornelius' daily tasks was milking the goats for the staff cups of tea.

rhesus monkeys, and three rare Soay sheep to enlarge the colony on Sheep Rock.

Apart from special attractions such as these, the Zoo's population was always undergoing change. Sometimes births produced surplus stock, which would be sold or exchanged, sometimes Sir Garrard would spot a good opportunity on the market and make a snap purchase. And he had an arrangement with London Zoo which was useful to both sides: they would send older animals to him, sometimes of species which otherwise he could not expect to acquire, and thus free their own space for younger beasts. Cobtree secured a variety of good quality animals, and because it was closed for several months each winter, the animals themselves enjoyed lives of semi-retirement which would have been impossible in Regents Park.

Red deer in a typical paddock.

After a quiet end to the 1948 season, the Zoo enjoyed a mercifully undisturbed winter: its first baby bison was born, the llamas were breeding prolifically, a pair of spotted hyenas and a chacma baboon were purchased, and the weather was kind. The new baboon was given a concrete based cage near Pets' Corner, behind which a rain shelter was built. A number of penny-in-the-slot machines, mostly of the pin-ball variety, and some of which accepted ha'pennies, were installed in the shelter. As is usually the case, they offered alluring prospects of winning something for next to nothing, but as is also usually the case, far more chances of losing your little all. They may have been a little down market for a serious establishment, but they brought the Zoo some useful additional revenue.

Television Comes to Cobtree

ALL was ready on March, 20th, 1949 for another opening day and another line up of celebrities. The stage as usual was set up near the baboon cage, facing the lions, and the season was inaugurated by Richard "Stinker" Murdoch, of the radio show, "Much Binding in the Marsh" — and famous many years later as Uncle Tom in I.T.V.'s "Rumpole of the Bailey". He was accompanied by his daughters, Jane and Belinda, who later opened Pets' Corner, and by Richard Hearne and John Snagge, famous radio and later T.V. sports commentator, both with their wives. Jane and Belinda's reward for cutting the ribbon across the entrance to Pets' Corner was an escorted walk with Enid Basnett through a private gate into Ronald White's leased paddock for a pony ride and some photographs. Meanwhile, Richard Hearne, as was his wont, entertained the crowds with some knock-about comedy, from which the Mayor and Mayoress of Maidstone, Cllr. and Mrs. Gordon Larking, who were also present, kept well clear. After he nearly lost his hat to a monkey who thought it looked tastier than the apple he offered it, he and the other stars obliged with handshakes and autographs until they were able to retreat to the Manor for the now statutory tea.

Easter was in mid-April that year, and the weather was fine; the Zoo enjoyed a bumper weekend, over 16,000 people paying for admission during the four days of the holiday. The staff were busy from morning till night, and there were queues for everything, including the toilets, which by the standards of the late twentieth century, were rather rudimentary, though at a time when many people still had earth closets at the bottom of their garden, they aroused no comment.

Sadly, a few weeks later, George Thorneycroft, the Head Keeper, was forced to retire because of ill health. He had been with Sir Garrard for 35 years, apart from the time he spent in the Forces during the First World War, had helped long ago with the travelling shows at Islington,

A typical scene on opening day.
Richard Murdoch and John Snagge almost engulfed by the crowds.

Crystal Palace, Southend, Margate and elsewhere, and had been Head Keeper since 1918. He was a first class all round keeper, but especially good with the lions: indeed, they never bred quite so freely after he had gone. He had lived on the estate throughout his long years of service, and continued to do so after his retirement.

Shortly after this took place, Nellie Durling left Cobtree. She had been a good and loyal worker — her epic walks to and from Chatham in the winter of 1947 were not quickly forgotten — but she felt it was time for a change of scene, so in the midst of a long, hot summer she said goodbye to Cobtree and set out for new worlds to conquer.

The weather encouraged huge crowds to visit the Zoo, and by the end of the season, over 100,000 people had paid for admission. On the final day, the last Sunday in October, Sir Garrard, who had, for the twelfth and final time, been elected Mayor of Maidstone, invited over 550 of the town's school children to Cobtree as a preliminary to National Savings Week. They had a fine time, with rides on the Royal Cream ponies, a chance to watch their Mayor feed his lions, and opportunities to ask him and his staff endless questions about the animals and the way in which the Zoo was run. The proceedings ended with tea, and as the children left, the gates of Cobtree closed for the winter.

When it re-opened, a new Head Keeper had been appointed to succeed George Thorneycroft. Winston Taylor came from Wilsons, a Glasgow firm of animal importers and dealers which also ran some small zoos and animal shows; he was specially experienced in the care of civets, weasel-like members of the cat family, and tropical fish, and brought with him a fund of new ideas for improving the Zoo and making it more attractive. It was indeed in need of fairly extensive renovation after over 10 years of minimal maintenance, but Sir Garrard was beginning to feel his years, and was reluctant to invest too heavily, so many of Taylor's proposals were never implemented.

At about the time Taylor arrived, Flossie Rayfield left the Zoo, first to visit the U.S.A. with her sister, and on her return, to take up much better paid work in Elliott's factory. She did not find factory life so rewarding as work at Cobtree, however, and in addition her health began to suffer: and some three years later she returned to Sir Garrard's service at the Zoo.

There had been little time in which to give effect to any of Winston Taylor's proposals by the time the 1950 opening day came round. Sir Garrard had, however, introduced one, rather low cost innovation: a fine stuffed lion (not one of the Zoo's; it is thought to have come from the Natural History Museum), which was set up in Ronald White's paddock before some metal grilles which were backed by a fine line of trees, to give the impression of a scene shot inside a cage. The effect was very realistic, and often there were queues of parents waiting to have their children photographed on the lion's back. There were no spoiled pictures, either — the lion never blinked or swished its tail at the wrong moment, unlike the wretched ponies.

Leslie Mitchell, newsreel, radio and T.V. commentator, did the honours on Opening Day. In introducing him, Sir Garrard recalled that many years before, when he had put on a show at Alexandra Palace, their duties had been reversed: Mitchell had then introduced him to the audience. Stage celebrities supporting the principal players included, once again, Richard Hearne and Yvonne Ortner, as well as Jeanne de Casalis, and others present included the Commander-in-Chief, The Nore, Admiral Sir Henry Moore, and the Mayor of Tonbridge, Miss Muriel Well. In his speech, Mitchell commented on the healthy appearance of the lions, which could be seen from the platform, and later, with Richard Hearne, he tried his hand at feeding them. Jeanne de Casalis entertained the large crowd with a Mrs. Feather monologue, and needless to say, the day ended for the distinguished guests over the teacups in the Manor House.

The summer was not so fine as in the previous year, but members of the Dickens Fellowship provided a little useful publicity in May when some of them arrived at the Zoo by coach and horses to visit Dingley Dell, which had been recreated in the lake area.

Sadly, in the same month, after an illness lasting over a year, George Thorneycroft died. He was not only a good keeper, but also a good and kind man, who had been loved and respected by all who knew him. He was greatly missed; and for Sir Garrard, his passing broke a link with his own youth.

Life at Cobtree went on however; in July, a litter of four wolf puppies was born, the first for several years, and one of the llamas had a black and white bull calf; in August, a very fine female Indian leopard was purchased, as well as a female chacma baboon from Africa, to provide a mate for the male already in residence, and finally as summer drew to a close, a young Grant's zebra arrived.

A visitor makes friends with a pony at the White Farmyard.

Although the weather had been poor, Sir Garrard reported another successful season when the Zoo closed in October; but as he grew older, he became ever more thrifty, and despite the efforts of his new Head Keeper and the entreaties of his staff, declined to spend an unnecessary penny as the new round of repainting and replacement got under way. Sometimes the staff laughed at his prudence, but most of them learned in time how to respond to it.

Nevertheless, Thelma recalls the efforts that were required to convince him that anything was worn out, and the time and labour that was wasted because of his reluctance to believe that buckets ever leaked. Buckets were very important at Cobtree, for hoses were used but sparingly, and in any case, there were only three stand-taps on the entire premises, one in the llamas' field, one by the parrot house, largely used by "Captain" Gates for his elephants, and one by the ladies toilets; and hot water could only be obtained from a tap outside the kitchen at the Manor House.

If the staff were unable to do as much as they would have wished during the winter, the Cobtree animals were as busy as ever. The most notable event was the birth of healthy twin cubs to one of Jack Kaye's charges, a European brown bear. Jack was a good all round keeper, but especially good with bears, and they did well throughout his stay at the Zoo.

As Spring approached, Sir Garrard announced to the staff that for the first time, television cameras would record the scene on Opening Day, and that in the following week it would be shown on Children's Newsreel. It is clear that his old showman's instincts remained as acute as ever: and the achievement was, of course, a considerable boost both for the Zoo and the County of Kent.

Sir Garrard was generally very weather-wise and picked sunny days for his Zoo's opening celebrations; unfortunately he chose wrongly this time, and it was showery on the day in March, 1951 when T.V. cameras first came to Cobtree. Eighteen year old Petula Clark made the first opening speech to reach a nationwide audience. She said that she hoped everyone, despite the wettish day, would enjoy themselves, and added that she had been promised a close quarters visit to the lions, and was not too sure if this was a good idea. Later she admitted that she had been terrified; but like a good trouper she had concealed her fear. She was supported on the platform by Leslie Mitchell and Richard Hearne, with whom she was co-starring in a film then in production. There was a sign of changing times in her outfit for the occasion: she was the first lady to officiate at a Cobtree opening not to wear a hat.

Zoo Plan

This plan is based on that published in 1949 although of course animals did change positions from time to time.

1	Sea and Water Birds	32	Parrot House
2	Big Birds	33	Birds of Prey
3	Small Water Birds	34	Kiosk
4	Rabbit Castle	35	Elephant House
5	Aviaries	36	Aviaries
6	Aviaries	37	Corner Paddock (later Dog Race Track)
7	Deer Paddock	38	Baboons and Chimpanzees
8	Llama Paddock	39	Coypus and Marmots
9	Deer Paddock	40	Pets' Corner and Children's Zoo
10	Emu Paddock	41	Otters
11	Rhea Paddock	42	Aquarium
12	Sarus Crane	43	Peccaries
13	Small Mammal House	44	Zoo Café
14	Beagles	45	Cub Enclosure (later Sea Lion Pool)
15	Fox Pen	46	Wild Sheep Rock
16	Wolves	47	The Pit
17	Bird Enclosure	48	Bear Cages
18	Bird Enclosure	49	Squirrel Cage
19	Husky Dog Enclosure	50	Monkey Cages
20	Wolf Enclosure	51	Goat Rock
21	Bird Enclosure	52	Monkey Cages
22	Wallaby Paddock	53	Round Stable
23	Dingoes	54	Lion and Tiger Terrace
24	Zebra and Antelope House	55	Small Mammal Enclosures
25	White Farmyard	56	Sunken Yard
26	Llamas and Cranes	57	Deer Enclosure
27	Aviaries	58	Bison
28	Cavey Village	59	Water Fowl
29	Small Carnivore Terrace	60	Budgerigars
30	Cattle Shed (original Elephant House)	61	Service Yard
31	Camel Yard		

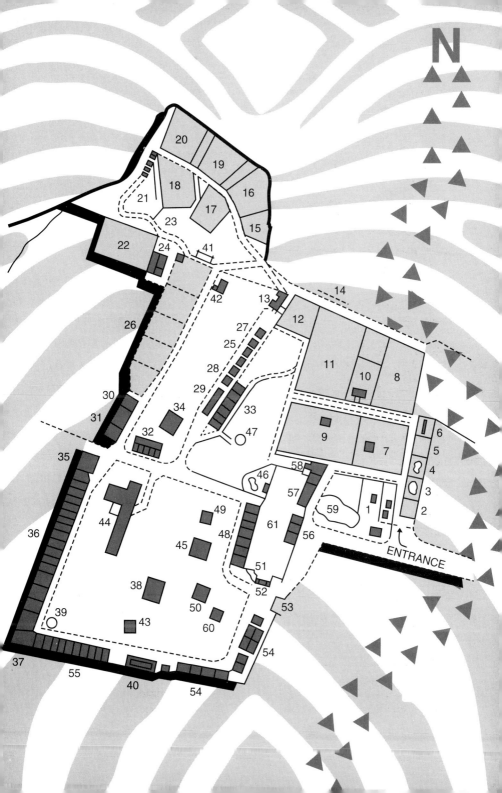

Petula Clark poses for the camera.

Over 1,000 visitors watched Petula's speech, but not all of them heard
it, for there were some technical problems, gremlins in the microphone
and some of the speakers, which Sir Garrard ascribed to "someone messing
about with them". Many, for the same reason, did not hear Richard Hearne
describe Petula as "the sweetest person he had ever worked with"; but
later, everyone saw Enid Basnett present her with a bouquet of spring
flowers at Pets' Corner. And at 5 o'clock one evening during the following
week, thousands both saw and heard the proceedings clearly, in the warmth
and comfort of their own front rooms. Sir Garrard, always a kindly man,
invited Enid to see herself on his set, for like many others in 1951, she
did not yet have a T.V. of her own.

Early in April, Lisa Daniely, French star of the film "Lilli Marlene",
visited Maidstone, and after touring the Tilling-Stevens bus works and
Edward Sharpe's toffee factory, lunched with a group of local celebrities
at the Royal Star Hotel. Afterwards she toured the Cobtree Zoo as the

guest of Sir Garrard and Lady Edna before going on to a gala performance of "Lilli Marlene" at the Granada Cinema.

Meanwhile, the bear cubs, encouraged by their mother, were beginning to venture out of the sleeping quarters where initially they had spent most of their time, and they rapidly became a popular attraction and in May some Soay and mouflon lambs were born, both breeds of wild sheep officially classified as rare. Some unusual hybrids also appeared at about this time.

June saw the arrival of Bertha, a 4½ year old chimpanzee bred at Edinburgh Zoo. It is not known if she was purchased or exchanged — Sir Garrard had long standing connections with Edinburgh — but it is recorded that she had been getting rather quarrelsome at home, and it was felt that a change of scene might be good for her. She settled down quickly at Maidstone, her acrobatics on a tree branch and an old tyre suspended in her cage soon establishing her as a popular favourite.

A little later, work was started on one of Winston Taylor's ideas for widening the Zoo's appeal. This was a small race track with boxes to house three dogs. A mechanical hare was installed, consisting of two sticks and a large feather fixed to a wire, and driven by an electric motor. This was housed in a pit dug in the ground, which was covered with corrugated iron when not in use. The control lever protruded above ground, so the starter (it was often Reg Yardley) could see what was going on. Built by members of the Cobtree staff, the track was ready shortly before the end of the season, and was shown to the public as a foretaste of some of the new attractions awaiting them next year.

As usual, the Zoo closed for the winter at the end of October, and Ronald White said goodbye to his friends on the staff at Cobtree, and to the Cream ponies and the stuffed lion which had served him so well for the past six years.

Lisa Daniely visits Pets' Corner.

His photographic business outside the Zoo had grown, and now demanded more of his time — latterly his wife, Mabel, had often stood in for him at Cobtree — and with new, improved, cameras beginning to come on to the market, and film at last freely available again, more visitors than before were taking their own photographs.

White went on to a successful career in commercial work and portraiture, becoming well known for his innovative wedding photographs, and in due course he was appointed an Associate of the Institute of British Photographers. One of his major commissions was to record the construction of the BP oil refinery at the Isle of Grain, where he had another opportunity to photograph Princess Elizabeth, who had meanwhile become the Queen. He did not entirely lose touch with Cobtree, however, for he was always there on Opening Day, taking pictures of the celebrities, which could be seen a few days later displayed in a showcase which he rented in Week Street, near to what was then Boots the Chemists, and is now W. H. Smith's bookshop.

The race track proved an instant success during its trial run, despite being much smaller than a normal dog track — the course measured only 70 yards, compared with the 500 yards of Rochester stadium — and after the Zoo had closed for the winter, work began on its completion. A fourth trap was built, a high fence, quite unlike the see-through fences Sir Garrard favoured elsewhere, was erected on the outer perimeter, so that no one could see what was going on from outside, and a motley collection of mongrel dogs of the terrier persuasion was acquired from Battersea Dogs Home.

The Zoo's animal stocks were now restored to something like their pre-war level, and more Royal visitors came to see them in November, when the Duke and Duchess of Gloucester brought the young Prince William on a private visit during his half-term holiday. They lunched with Sir Garrard and Lady Edna before being conducted around the grounds. Prince William was particularly intrigued with Wolf Wood, and Sir Garrard as usual on such occasions, carried with him a chip-basket of titbits so that members of the Royal party could feed some of the animals if they wished.

The remainder of the winter passed uneventfully, except for a short scare in February when foot and mouth disease broke out at Rochester Meadow Farm, which adjoined Cobtree; fortunately, however, the Zoo was not affected, and all was ready for another opening day on 23rd March, 1952.

Richard Hearne attempting to get the dogs started.

Television cameras were again on hand as the nation's leading radio and T.V. commentator, Richard Dimbleby, made the inaugural speech. At that period he was hosting a popular radio programme called "Down Your Way", which went out at about the same time, so many people had to choose which version of Dimbleby they wanted. The personal appearance clearly won, for there was a huge crowd to hear him describe Sir Garrard as a "remarkable man who has been Mayor of Maidstone so often that it seems as if the appointment has become automatic: he has kept a collection of wild animals for over 50 years and been bitten more often than he can remember, yet still keeps the collection so that others can see, study and enjoy it".

Comedian, Leslie Henson and his wife, as well as the ever loyal Richard Hearne and Yvonne Ortner, were also on the platform, Henson, and Hearne in his guise as Mr. Pastry, entertaining the crowds with some comedy turns during the tour of the Zoo which followed the speeches. The Hearne's seven year old daughter, Sarah, opened Pets' Corner, admission to which was now 6d. (2½p) for adults and 3d. for children, and the final ceremony took place at the new race track, which was opened by Mr. Pastry.

The T.V. cameras had a field day here, for the ex-Battersea mongrels had not learnt the finer arts of racing, and some fought each other instead of pursuing the hare, one easily outstripped it, and then waited patiently for it to catch up with him before resuming the chase, and another, with no idea of what was required of him, simply ran enthusiastically round and round the track, wagging his tail and barking, and paying no attention either to the hare or the other dogs. Richard Hearne, already a seasoned T.V. performer, got very involved, and was thus unable to sign autographs in the time honoured way; learning of the disappointment this had caused, he wrote a letter to the local newspaper, giving his address, and promising that he would sign and return a blank sheet of paper that any child cared to send to him.

Only a week later, the South of England was hit by the worst gale in living memory, but the Zoo escaped serious damage, and the Easter weekend, another two weeks later, found everything in order. The weather

Fun with the llama.
Enid Basnett (left) and Dinah Tanner attempt to get a reluctant llama under way.

was warm and sunny, and brought large crowds to Cobtree, which shared with the Navy Day at Chatham Dockyard, the best attendance figures for any event in Kent.

Towards the end of April a new and unique attraction arrived at the Zoo. This was a Pere David's stag, from the only herd of these animals then in existence. Pere David's deer, distinguished by their long, mule-like tails, were originally kept in the grounds of the Imperial Palace in Peking,

. . . . if pushing and pulling won't work — try riding it!

*Some of the domestic animals were
as popular as the wild ones.*

but during the Boxer rebellion they escaped and were almost exterminated. A few were rescued and found a home at Woburn Abbey, seat of the Dukes of Bedford, from whence Cobtree's specimen came. Now, there are again, a few in China, for in 1987 the present Duke returned some to their homeland where it is hoped that they will re-establish the breed.

The teething troubles of the race track were meanwhile being tackled and Diana Taylor, who had previously worked at Rochester Greyhound Stadium, was engaged to look after the dogs and traps. The dogs were slowly learning that they were supposed to chase the hare and not to eat it if they caught it, or to fight among themselves over it; and the mechanism controlling it was being modified so that the wire did not come off the guide wheels quite so often. No way of quenching the uproar the dogs made when being prepared for racing was found, but this proved to be no disadvantage, since it often attracted the curious in to see what was happening.

The race track created a lot of extra work; dogs had to be rounded up for each race, attempts made to prevent them getting at the hare, and fights brought to a conclusion as quickly as possible. Overall, however, it proved a very good investment and hundreds of visitors happily paid the extra 3d. (1¼p) which was charged for admission, many of them apparently enjoying the occasional contretemps as much as the racing.

For many years Sir Garrard had continued his experimental cross-breeding programme and in 1952 produced two more unusual animals: one was a hybrid yak, the result of crossing a yak and a Red Dexter cow, the other a wild pig, the product of crossing an Indian wild boar with a Tamworth sow, and then putting a female from the resultant litter back to the boar.

Daisy Runs Amok

AFTER over twelve years at the Zoo, Enid Basnett, who meanwhile had married, decided that it was time to retire, and she left in July. The work was demanding and the hours, she recalls, were long. The men started at 7.30 in the morning, the women at 8.30, and everyone continued until after closing time. This meant in summer rarely leaving before 7.30 p.m., and frequently later, while even in winter it was not often possible to get away before 5 o'clock. Furthermore, the staff had to work a six day week in summer and alternately six and five day weeks in winter and no one got both Christmas Day and Boxing Day off in the same season. Now Enid felt that it was time to devote a little more of her attention to her husband and home.

She had thoroughly enjoyed her life at Cobtree; she had been with the Zoo through all the difficult years of the war and its aftermath, had seen countless youngsters, many of them girls straight from school, join the staff and leave, some after only a few weeks, and had witnessed the arrival and departure of hundreds of animals. She recalls the joy felt at a successful birth among the inmates, the misery of cold, dark, winter days in wartime, when the difficulties of keeping going seemed almost insurmountable, and the pleasure and sense of achievement of warm summer days when the war was over and the Zoo was full of happy crowds and well cared for animals. She recalls also moments of high comedy when nimble-footed goats and sheep escaped and defied all efforts to recapture them, and stubborn animals declined to carry out their intended duties, often to the delight of visitors who showed little sympathy for their unfortunate keepers.

Over the years Sir Garrard had learned to respect Enid's views about the way in which Pets' Corner should be run, as well as on broader questions concerning the Zoo. He sometimes even bowed to her criticism of his spelling, which was not very good. On one occasion she remembers pointing out to him that a new sign he had done, and which was already erected on one of the cages, contained a mistake. "No one will notice", he replied, but Enid stuck to her guns. "I did", she pointed out, and Sir Garrard accepted defeat, took the sign down and repainted it. He demanded hard work from all his staff, Enid recalls, and the pay was low; but he was always ready to give a hand at difficult times, and never too proud to have a mug of tea and a chat with his people during breaks in the work.

The entrance to Pets' Corner.

Soon after Enid left, Mary Thackary and Brian Smith joined the staff, Mary to help at Pets' Corner and with the small mammals generally, Brian to assist "Captain" Gates as an elephant boy. Later he undertook sheep shearing, and looked after the zebra and mule, and some cows. Although Mary stayed for only a few years, leaving Cobtree to join the Metropolitan Police, she was unlucky enough on one occasion to be bitten in the calf by an American wild pig, or peccary, while cleaning out his cage. Help was quickly forthcoming — the cage was near Pets' Corner — but Mary was left with a scar on her leg as a permanent reminder of the event. Brian was a very fit young man, who walked every day to work from Coxheath. Although his starting time was 7.30 a.m., he soon found that if he arrived at Cobtree at about 7.00 a.m., he got a free breakfast. A pinch of Sir Garrard's snuff was another perk that came his way from time to time. He recalls that when Tyrwhitt-Drake entered the elephant house for the daily inspection his greeting was invariably "Good morning, Gates, good morning, boy". Indeed, Brian cannot recall Sir Garrard ever addressing him in any other way.

Foot and mouth disease was still affecting the neighbourhood in August, but Cobtree remained free of the disease. The following month, however, disaster of another kind hit the Zoo. One day, as Daisy the elephant was being led from her cage to the meadow behind the elephant house, a jet plane flew low overhead and frightened her. Although she was now 22 years old, she took her two-ton self off like a bullet from a gun, crashing through a fence into the adjoining wood, and stampeding through it unhindered by either the undergrowth or the young trees in her way, all of which she flattened like ninepins.

It is said that an elephant never forgets — perhaps Daisy was remembering the days of her childhood, when she followed her mother through the Burmese jungle; in any event, when she came to the end of the wood she was confronted by a steep clay bank, and without a pause attempted to climb it. The clay was slippery, however, and Daisy could not get a hold: she fell, and slid on her side to the bottom of the slope, fortunately suffering no damage in the process.

She now seemed totally traumatised, and to the dismay of Sir Garrard and other members of the staff who had hurried to the scene, declined to make any effort to get up. Hay and straw and other tempting eatables were brought and offered to her without effect, her companion Gert was fetched and led up and down nearby: Daisy was not interested, and continued to lie where she had fallen.

Like other animals, an elephant that cannot or will not get up can die quite quickly, so while a block and tackle were being erected on the site in the hope of lifting Daisy to her feet, an urgent request for help was taken in Sir Garrard's Rolls Royce to a circus currently playing at Canterbury which had a particularly good elephant trainer on its staff. Some say it was Sir Robert Fossett's Circus, others that it was Billy Smart's; nobody is sure, but Billy Smart did come to Maidstone a few weeks later, so it is probable that he was in the area at the time.

Mother llama proudly guards her baby . . . .

. . . . but Thelma was a trusted friend.

Before anyone could arrive from Canterbury, Daisy was in fact winched to her feet; but she did not like the indignity at all, immediately tossed the equipment aside, and went crashing once more into the wood. This time, really angry, she charged at anyone who tried to approach her, and as evening approached, Sir Garrard knew that he had a painful decision to take.

Although it was a tempting idea, he could not risk leaving Daisy in the wood all night in the hope that by morning she would have calmed down: there was too great a danger that she might escape and seriously hurt someone, or if not that, at least cause immense damage either inside or outside the Zoo. His men were becoming exhausted, and he could not hope to mount an effective guard over the whole wood throughout the night. With great reluctance, therefore, he ordered guns to be prepared; the normally good natured Daisy would have to be put down.

She must have sensed that time was up. Just before the fatal shots were to be fired, as dusk was falling, Daisy recovered her composure, and quietly allowed "Captain" Gates to lead her back to the elephant house and bed her down, as if nothing out of the ordinary had happened all day.

The remainder of the season passed mercifully without further excitement. It had been a good one for Sir Garrard; Cobtree offered excellent value for money, the admission charge remaining only 1/6d. (7½p), compared for example with prices ranging from 2/6d. (12½p) to 10/6d. (52½p) for a seat at Billy Smart's Circus when it came to Maidstone that Autumn. And a visit to the Cobtree race track offered additional entertainment at a bargain price; by the time the gates closed in October, nearly 20,000 spectators had paid to watch the dogs.

During the winter, Arthur Carter arrived at Cobtree; he remained until the end, and although engaged specifically to look after the bears, he was a good all-round keeper and at times helped with all the animals in the Zoo. Soon after his arrival, a North African miniature donkey, the smallest breed of donkey in the world, produced a foal, and a Tibetan yak was purchased. Tim o'Timilee died, and his grieving owners had him stuffed and mounted, and took him back to the home he had outgrown when alive. It seems that they donated the substantial cage they had paid to have built for him to Sir Garrard, for an exceptionally large tiger named Rajah was secured, and installed in it before the 1953 season began.

There were a few hours of anxiety in February, not long before the opening date, when violent storms and high tides resulted in serious flooding in the South East. Many coastal areas were inundated, and rivers burst their banks, many lives and much livestock being lost; but the high ground on which Cobtree stood saved the Zoo, and all was ready on March 22nd, a lovely, early spring day, when actress Vanessa Lee arrived to inaugurate the 1953 season.

Miss Lee was accompanied by her husband, singing teacher Ward Morgan, and Richard Hearne, opposite whom she had been playing in pantomime at the London Palladium, as well as by Arthur Brough and his wife. Brough's repertory company was playing successfully at the time at Maidstone's Palace Theatre, which stood in Gabriel's Hill, and was later pulled down to make way for a shop, initially Sainsbury's and now a branch of Robert Dyas the ironmongers.

There was a slight change to the usual programme on this occasion: Vanessa Lee and the rest of the platform party were conducted round the Zoo before the opening ceremony instead of after it. Vanessa was particularly intrigued by the elephants, Gert and Daisy. Gert spotted an apple in the actress' hand, opened her mouth and lifted her trunk to receive it; Vanessa threw and missed, so that Gert had to stoop and probe around to locate it. Richard Hearne then demonstrated his superior skill, acquired with years of practice, by throwing a slice of bread to her and landing it precisely on her tongue.

As Mr. Pastry, he went on to open the dog track, offering a delighted crowd a long programme of clowning. Before one race started, he lay face down along the near side of one of the hurdles, so that the dogs had to jump over him as well as the fence. They all made it successfully except for Tail-end Charlie, toiling along well behind the rest of the field. Mr. Pastry did not see him coming, and thinking that all the dogs had passed, began to rise to his feet. The dog was as shocked as Mr. P. when he collided with the comedian's stomach, sending himself rolling in the dust and Mr. P's spectacles and bowler hat flying through the air in different directions.

Mr. Pastry did not easily admit defeat, however, and was soon back in action, challenging the winner of the Cobtree Stakes to a race for a bottle of champagne presented by Vanessa Lee. To improve his speed, Mr. P. removed his shoes, revealing a fine pair of bottle green socks; surprisingly, he and the terrier (a dog of uncertain breed) got off to a good start when the hare hove into view, but sadly thereafter the accepted rules of racing were not strictly observed. Mr. P. in particular was noticed on several occasions to be cutting corners, but his efforts proved unavailing, and the dog ended a clear winner. Both parties expressed satisfaction, however, after the presentations had been made. The terrier generously gave Mr. Pastry the champagne he had won in exchange for the outsize bone awarded to the runner-up. Mr. P. may well have felt that he had earned his tea by the time he got to the Manor with the rest of the guests. It was, presumably, felt that the dog had had his day, for he was not invited.

Admission charges went up to 2/- (10p) for the new season, and pony rides now cost 6d., but the price for children remained unchanged at 9d. and the prices for admission to the special enclosures, Pets' Corner, the aquarium, and the dog track, also remained unaltered, as did the cost of a programme. For 3d. the visitor now got a much thicker book than the thin and flimsy wartime production. It was printed by Esgate, Chamberlain & Co. of Maidstone, who did the job throughout the Zoo's existence. There was a map on the centre pages, and a walk-through guide to the Zoo, with details of the animals encountered to right and left as the walk was followed. And advertising was again included.

Pony rides were always popular.

Among the regular advertisers were Maidstone Gas Company, later succeeded by the South Eastern Gas Board, both proud to inform the world that all the cooking at Cobtree was done by gas; Sergeant and Parks Ltd., who were equally proud to point out that they supplied all the paint used at the Zoo, and Dennis Paine & Company, who supplied fencing for all purposes, including zoological ones. Style & Winch, Sir Garrard's firm, not surprisingly, always took space to inform visitors that they supplied soft drinks and mineral waters to the Zoo's catering establishments, while Corfe & Company, chemists, offered roll film and a developing and printing service to visitors through the same establishments.

Other regular advertisers included Rootes and H. J. Pocock & Sons, both motor dealers; George H. Leavey & Company, outfitters; J. A. S. Smith Ltd., timber merchants; Houghams, bakers and Frank Cassell, fishmonger. Sharps, the famous toffee people, deserve a special mention. Not only were they regular advertisers, but their emblem, a macaw, which was known all over the country, was based on a photograph of a bird hired from Sir Garrard. Not surprisingly, it featured in all their advertisements in the programme.

The season was still young when, on May 4th, everyone at the Zoo was saddened by the sudden death of Daisy the elephant. Brian Smith found her lying on her side when he came in the morning to the cage she shared with Gert. He knew at once that something was wrong, for she normally slept while standing. There was no evident cause of death and it was assumed that a heart attack was responsible. For many years she had a broken tusk, from which it was thought she suffered considerably at times, but it is unlikely that this contributed directly to her death. Perhaps the stampede she engaged in the previous year had done her more harm than was appreciated at the time.

Sir Garrard, who normally never missed out on a chance of a new story, sent no report of the tragedy to the press; he was seventy-two years old now, and perhaps felt that in losing Daisy he had lost an old friend. Consequently, many visitors to Cobtree remained unaware that Daisy had gone. It was, after all, not uncommon to see only one elephant in the house; the other might be out in the orchard being exercised or being washed down. And Gert continued to entertain, pushing her trunk through the bars of the cage in search of buns, gathering dust from the floor and blowing it out over the watching crowds or, while being washed down by "Captain" Gates, removing his hat and waving it around out of his reach: she had a more vivid sense of humour than her lost companion.

A young intruder feeds the wallabies.

Two uneventful months followed Daisy's death; then one evening in July, two wallabies felt a sudden urge to see the world, and managed to escape from their enclosure. One hopped out into the headlights of a Maidstone and District bus in Forstal Road, giving the startled driver just time to stop without hitting it, and then sat down to await developments. The bus driver and some of his passengers, including an off duty policeman, got down and cautiously approached the animal, which must have been feeling rather unsure of itself, for they quite quickly managed to surround and capture it (the policeman's cape came in very handy), after which they returned it through the main entrance to the Manor House, which was not far away. The other wallaby had disappeared, and it was thought useless to search for it in the dark — it was 11 p.m. when the escape was discovered, and wallabies are not dangerous beasts. It was found next morning in the woods adjoining its enclosure, having been content simply to check up on the greenness of the grass on the other side of the fence. It was easily recovered and put back among its companions.

August Bank Holiday weekend was fine and warm, and resulted in good business for the Zoo and its café and ice cream kiosks: it is recorded that Style and Winch had stacks of crates of empty lemonade bottles to collect the following week, and that large numbers of wasps were attracted by the plenitude of sticky mouths, fingers and dropped cornets on offer.

The Bank Holiday takings no doubt played their part in enabling Sir
Garrard to announce another successful season as the time for the winter
closure approached; and he confirmed that he expected to re-open the Zoo
again in March, 1954.

Meanwhile he spent a busy winter. Just before Christmas he took
part, with the 83 year old actor Bransby Williams, in a discussion on the
B.B.C. Light Programme of the works of Charles Dickens, during which
he claimed that Cobtree was the inspiration for Dingley Dell in "Pickwick
Papers". Possibly stretching his remit slightly, but as ever, not missing a
chance to promote his Zoo, he mentioned that the Manor House was more
than 400 years old, and that it crossed the borders of two parishes, Boxley
and Allington. Indeed, he said, "You are sitting in Boxley, Mr. Williams,
and I am sitting in Allington", which was not strictly true, although it
would have been until some 20 years earlier, when a local government
boundary revision had placed all of the Manor in the parish of Boxley.

Christmas had been a busy season for Sir Garrard almost without a
break since the time during the First World War when he supplied ponies
to the World Fair in Islington, and it remained so still. Strictly speaking,
of course, his ponies were not part of the Zoo, but it is doubtful if the
Cobtree staff noticed the difference. At Christmas, 1953, he supplied four
Royal Creams, with a handler whose name is recorded only as Jean, to
draw Cinderella's coach, which he also provided, in the pantomime at the
London Palladium. Julie Andrews was playing the starring role, and
became very interested in the little creatures. One of them, well known
for her docility and good temper, was in foal; but despite this, she performed
faultlessly throughout the long season.

Meanwhile, maintenance and replacement went on as usual at the
Zoo. It was decided that new enclosures were needed for the porcupines
and coypus; both of these are burrowers, so the male staff had to mix and
lay substantial concrete bases for them, while for the coypus, which are
swimmers, and had grown into a sizeable colony, a small pool had also to
be provided.

Outside work was brought to a halt in February, however, by the
onset of the coldest weather since the great freeze-up of 1947. The temperature fell to −19°F, and watering the animals became a matter of great
difficulty. The lake by the main entrance in Chatham Road froze hard,
and attracted many skaters during the first weekend of the cold spell;
fortunately, unlike Mr. Pickwick, none of them fell in. Then, mercifully,

Winston Taylor operating the "hare" mechanism at the Dog Track.

the weather eased, so that despite the delays, the new enclosures were finished, and all was ready when the time for the next opening came round.

It was a warm March day with a feeling of Spring in the air when Julie Andrews, Jeanne de Casalis and other celebrities arrived to watch a new innovation at a Cobtree Opening Day. For the first time, the ceremony was performed by the current Mayor of Maidstone who, in 1954, was 82 year old Alderman Thomas Armstrong. Perhaps he had expressed a personal wish to Sir Garrard to undertake the duty; at any rate, in his speech he referred, flatteringly, to the owner of the Zoo as a "great showman" and added that "now he has the oldest Mayor in England appearing for him". The occasion had another, special, significance, for it signalled the start of Cobtree's 21st season. Truly, Maidstone Zoo had grown up.

Julie Andrews expressed a special wish to see the little mare which had helped to draw her carriage while pregnant in the pantomime at the London Palladium, and which, meanwhile, had given birth to a healthy foal. So after the speeches, the platform party visited the stables, and Julie, with the aid of some Kent cider, appropriately christened the new baby, "Cinders".

The party then went on to visit some of the Zoo's favourite inmates, including Gert, the surviving elephant, the second chimp to be named Martha, the polar bears Sam and Barbara, Cæsar and Sheila the lions and, of course, the Pere David stag, before pausing to admire the new porcupine and coypu enclosures. Finally they reached the dog track, which Jeanne

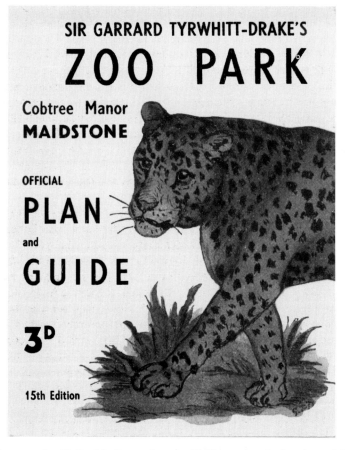

Guide cover for 1948. Sir Garrard was still illustrating the brochures himself.

de Casalis opened in her role as Mrs. Feather. Five chaotic races were staged before the visitors retreated to the Manor for the usual restoring tea.

Admission charges remained unchanged for 1954; but there was a way of getting into the Zoo free, and even earning a little money as well, which John Anderson remembers. Sir Garrard would pay 1/- (5p) for each small animal or snake brought to the Zoo, and admit the finder free of charge for the rest of the day. John spent many hours as a lad on the banks of the River Medway searching for his reward and free ticket, and in fact captured many grass snakes. But he had a fatal weakness, he would stop to eat his dinner before going to the Zoo with his prize and, time after time, found that, while he was eating, his slithery prisoner had escaped from the jam jar which he used for holding his catches. Only once did he avoid this misfortune, and he remembers to this day, the joyous afternoon he spent roaming the Zoo after claiming the shilling reward for his find.

Easter was in the second week of April that year, and there were some interesting and unusual newcomers at Cobtree for the holiday visitors to see. Mary, the brown bear had given birth to another pair of twins, which looked exactly like the teddy bears beloved of all children. She was a good mother, and did not let her babies out of her sight for a moment, nor did she allow the public to look at them for too long at a time. After permitting them to play for a little while on the slopes of Bear Terrace she would usher them back to the privacy of the nursery, and they would not appear again until she thought the time was ripe.

A rare event was the birth of a son to Celia, a rhesus monkey from India. Like all of his kind, he had the wrinkled face of a grandfather when young; but no one could mistake him for anything but a baby, for he clung to his mother almost continuously for the first two months of his life, even when she was hanging upside down from the top of her cage, or leaping, miraculously it seemed, from bough to bough of the tree inside it.

These were, so to speak, special births. But spring had seen the usual crop of normal arrivals at the Zoo — llamas, ponies, rabbits and so on — and to see all these, and to learn at first hand of Sir Garrard's achievements in wild animal preservation and breeding, an impressive party of top rank Zoologists visited Cobtree in May. From the Zoological Society of London came Dr. L. Harrison Matthews, from Whipsnade Zoo came Mr. E. Tong, from Dublin, Mr. C. Webb and from Bristol, Mr. R. Creed. Mr. D. Bowles represented Edinburgh Zoo, and Mr. B. McLean, Belfast, while Mr. G. Mottershead represented Chester Zoo. Winston Taylor joined the party for lunch at the Manor before Sir Garrard took the visitors on a tour

Jeanne de Casalis gets two of the dogs away in good order.
The man behind the traps is Martin Hammond a long term supporter of the Zoo.

Flat out in the dog races.
The "flying feather" masquerading as the hare can be seen in the foreground.

of his establishment, which many of them may have compared unfavourably with their own larger undertakings. Indeed, in some zoological circles, Cobtree was referred to as "The Packing Case Zoo". The fact is however, that Tyrwhitt-Drake's record in animal health and breeding success compared favourably with all of them.

An advertising float ready to join Maidstone Carnival.
In charge, left to right, are Nellie Durling, Betty Cheyney and Flossie Rayfield.

In June, an old friend returned to the Zoo. Richard Hearne had been on tour in the U.S.A., and had also done some very successful TV shows there. Now he wanted to see the baby bears and the young rhesus monkey, and to visit the dogs in their kennels. As Mr. Pastry, he challenged any of Sir Garrard's beasts to beat his own lively terrier twice round the dog track, and a large crowd flocked in to see the fun, but sadly, the result of the race is not known. As he left, Mr. Pastry announced that it would be a while before he was seen again in the Maidstone area, for following his recent successes in the U.S.A., he would soon be going back there.

The remainder of the summer was not very eventful. The parrot house, which contained mainly cockatoos, macaws and parrots, found itself uncomfortably full following the donation of a collection of parrots which had possibly belonged to the landlady of The Ship public house which stood at the bottom of Gabriels Hill. This lady also had a monkey which is believed to have gone to the Zoo; but it is not absolutely certain whether the birds given to Sir Garrard at this time came from her or from some other, unknown, resident of Maidstone.

Early in the autumn, Brian Smith received his call-up papers, and reluctantly left Cobtree to do his National Service. He never returned, for in the forces he learned another trade, and on his release embarked on a new career in a completely different field. His love of large beasts seems never to have left him, however, for today he is the owner of several superb traction engines.

Towards the end of October, Sir Garrard announced that he proposed to build a sea lions enclosure during the winter, and that opening day in 1955 would be March 20th. Then Cobtree grew quiet once more, apart from the noises of the animals and the sounds of repair work and renovation in progress. Some delay to the winter programme was caused by heavy snow in January, however, and this also led to the escape of one of the wolves.

One day towards the end of the month, the weight of snow on the six foot high fence surrounding Wolf Wood, which had a three foot wide overhang at the top, caused a section to collapse. One of the wolves, which had been born in the Zoo, seized the chance to walk out, and it set off on a gentle amble through the 300 acres of the Cobtree estate.

Its escape was soon noticed, and armed with guns, Sir Garrard, with Winston Taylor and Arthur Carter, set out in pursuit, guided by the animal's footprints in the snow. The going was hard, and Sir Garrard, who was now 73, had to give up after a while and leave the pursuit to Taylor and Carter. After some three hours of trekking, the two men cornered the wolf, which had managed to get through the boundary fence, just outside the estate.

It was, in fact, unlikely to cause any harm; but at that time tranquilising darts had not been introduced, and the risk of losing it on public land could not be taken, so sadly Mr. Taylor had to shoot it. It was the last of the Russian wolves, for its parents had died some time previously, and it had no brothers or sisters; Wolf Wood was not left empty, however, for the Zoo still had some North American wolves and dingoes.

Outdoor work resumed when the snow cleared, and among the later jobs completed that winter was the building of a concrete pool for a fine three year old female Californian sea lion which Sir Garrard had purchased.

This was built on the site of the former cub enclosure opposite Goat Rock and the bear cages.

While the male staff completed their winter maintenance work, the female employees carried on with their traditional winter tasks of painting, the weeding of the footpaths, and the tidying up of the verges. Most of them found the work very tedious, although Enid Basnett recalls that she always enjoyed it — it was a restful job, she says. The original wooden seats which dotted the grounds had by now all been replaced with concrete ones, and everyone was glad that these at least required little or no attention from year to year.

The snow was all gone, the sun shining, and B.B.C. Television cameras on hand, when Richard Hearne, back again from the States, who had visited Cobtree so often but only once previously performed the opening ceremony, did so for the second time on March 20th, 1955. He was attired in Mr. Pastry's famous bowler hat and baggy suit, and as usual entertained the crowd with his much loved combination of slapstick comedy and witty dialogue, which as always was delivered with superb timing.

Several favourites from earlier days returned to Cobtree to join Hearne on the platform that day. They included his wife, Yvonne Ortner and their children, Cetra and Sarah, the veteran music hall stars Elsie and Doris Waters, and Stanley Holloway, who had opened the last pre-war season, and his wife. The Mayor and Mayoress of Maidstone were, as usual, also on the platform — that year Alderman A. H. Clark and Mrs. Clark.

In his speech, Hearne briefly dropped his Mr. Pastry identity, and spoke of the great happiness he and his family had experienced at Cobtree with Sir Garrard and Lady Edna, and among the animals; then he became Mr. Pastry once more, and declared the Zoo well and truly open. After this Cetra and Sarah presented bouquets to the ladies — a task often carried out in the past before the ceremony by the Head Keeper at the private gate through which the platform party normally entered the Zoo. Then everyone went walkabout.

There was a long halt at the new sea lion enclosure, for the Zoo had never had a sea lion before. Sir Garrard mentioned that Stanley Holloway knew something about zoos — he was referring of course to his still famous story of "Albert and the Lion" — and invited him to christen the Zoo's newest inmate. Holloway obliged, and appropriately named her Albertina.

At last the party moved on to the dog track, where Mr. Pastry once again officiated, challenging a border terrier to a race, in which at first he ran in the wrong direction, and then fell over the last hurdle, so that, in full view of the television cameras, the dog finally won a famous victory.

Soon after the start of the season, Sir Garrard made another purchase, a 25 year old double-humped Bactrian camel named Bill, thus filling a gap in the Zoo's animal collection which had lasted for several years. Bill was given a home adjacent to the original elephant house; he had a taste for hats, and sometimes removed an especially attractive one from a visitor's head, causing some agitation in consequence. Following his arrival, the summer progressed without incident until August, when there was an unfortunate accident.

Tea, but not at the Manor, for Mr. Pastry.

One afternoon, a family from Southborough approached the lions' cages a little while before feeding time, and sat down on the grass to await the keeper's arrival. One of the daughters, a little girl four years old, wandered off towards the rhesus monkeys' cage. Her father, noticing that she had vanished, looked round and saw to his horror that she was climbing the safety barrier in front of the cage. He hurried towards her, but before he could reach her, she leaned forward to touch the outstretched arm of one of the monkeys. As she did so, another monkey hurled itself against the cage, causing the wire mesh to bend, and bit the first finger of the child's left hand.

The little girl was taken to West Kent General Hospital for initial treatment, and later was given a skin graft at the Royal Victoria Hospital at East Grinstead. After the Zoo had closed for the winter in October at the end of another successful season, Sir Garrard tried, with the aid of his chauffeur's 4½ year old daughter (but no monkeys) to work out what had happened. The little girl proved quite incapable of reaching the top of the safety barrier without adult help, and even when there, could not reach or even touch the mesh of the cage, which was three feet from the barrier, without losing her balance. Furthermore, the mesh was far too fine for any monkey to push its head through. How the accident happened thus remained a mystery, but as a precaution an extra barrier was erected. And the following year, the child was awarded £150 damages against Sir Garrard.

Only one noteworthy event took place during the winter; this was in February when the Duke and Duchess of Gloucester paid a second visit to Cobtree, this time bringing Prince Richard with them. The Royal party were joined by Sir Malcolm Sargent, a personal friend, and Sir John Ferguson, the Chief Constable of Kent, for lunch with Sir Garrard and Lady Edna at the Manor before they were conducted round the Zoo. Prince Richard asked many questions about the animals, and wanted to know if there were any new ones. Sir Garrard told him that there were indeed many newcomers, and that the latest was a male Malayan tiger which was still unnamed: perhaps the Prince could suggest a name for him? The Prince could, and did, and so before the Royal visitors left at dusk, the tiger had become Richard.

On March 18th, 1956, nearly one thousand people assembled before the familiar platform — it was mounted on wheels and had been used for years — which was placed, as usual, near the lion cages, to watch the

Sir Garrard introduces Sir Alfred Bossom, M.P., on Opening Day 1956. In the background is the café.

opening ceremony. On the platform with Sir Garrard and Lady Edna were Elsie and Doris Waters, Richard Hearne, Sir Alfred Bossom, M.P., Brigadier Harold Fletcher, Mayor of Maidstone, who declared the Zoo open, and the Mayoress, Mrs. Irene Gibbons. Jeanne de Casalis had hoped to attend, but was unable to do so, and sent her apologies and best wishes.

Following the precedent set in 1953, the platform party had been shown round much of the Zoo before the opening ceremony, and after the speeches were over, it repaired at once to the dog track, which Mr. Pastry opened in his customary manner. There was keen competition among the press photographers covering the event for good positions from which to record Mr. P's acrobatics, so much so that several had to move rather sharply to avoid closer contact with him or one of the dogs than they had intended. The crowd were offered the customary five races before Sir Garrard's guests retired for another celebratory tea at the Manor, delayed en route by the usual bevy of autograph hunters and by a special detour to admire Richard, the new tiger.

At about this time "Yank" Miller, who was actually a Canadian, joined the staff to mainly look after the big cats. He had worked in circuses in the States before coming to England, and afterwards had been with Bostocks, Chapmans, Robert Brothers and other circuses in this country as a trainer and keeper before he decided to retire from circus life and settle at Cobtree.

Miller brought valuable experience in the teatment of sick animals with him, the more useful at the time, since existing methods of veterinary treatment, particularly of large exotic animals, were still relatively primitive: several years were still to pass before David Taylor's pioneering research began to bring about a real improvement.

Sir Garrard, of course, had much practical experience in dealing with sick animals, including that which he had gained while serving in the Veterinary Corps during the First World War. There was a hospital at Cobtree, a wooden building which became hot in summer and cold in winter, so when possible, most sick animals were kept in their sleeping quarters. The keepers all had their own preferred remedies, Fred Youell, the stud groom, being the recognised specialist for illnesses affecting the hoofed animals. Under Sir Garrard's general guidance, a limited number of well tried remedies were usually applied in the first instance to animals which fell ill or were injured, and only when these failed, and then only in the case of rare or valuable beasts, was the expense of calling a vet considered. Usually the vet, when he came, could do little more than

Arthur Carter introduces his kitten to Martha.

confirm the Zoo's own treatment, and perhaps occasionally prescribe drugs which could not be obtained across the counter. Some cunning was often needed to get animals to take such medicine as was available. That for lions was packed inside a small parcel of meat tied up with sewing cotton; the lion swallowed the meat whole, unaware of what it contained and the cotton did no damage.

Sir Garrard was elected Chairman of the Zoological Society of London in 1956, and his Zoo enjoyed a successful but uneventful summer. The winter which followed was also quiet, apart from one dramatic afternoon in January when two lions escaped. Cæsar and Mary, who lived in one of the large concrete based enclosures, had been shut in their sleeping quarters, as was usual, while the front of their pen was cleaned. About midday the keeper who was carrying out the work took his lunch break, and on his return, having finished work in the front of the pen, released the two animals into it, so that he could clean out the rear. As they emerged, he went in to start work, not realising that he had not fastened the door in the front of the cage.

Cæsar and Mary walked through it unobserved, and were not seen for some time. Then Nellie Durling and another keeper named Margaret

Holland saw them roaming in the park, and hurried to tell Sir Garrard the bad news. He gathered together all the male keepers, and together they set out to try to recapture the two beasts. It proved impossible, however; the light was poor, the early winter dusk was rapidly approaching, and Mary was a bad-tempered animal at the best of times.

Reluctantly, Sir Garrard decided that to prevent any danger of the animals escaping into the outside world during the night, Mary would have to be shot — there were still no anaesthetic darts, the use of which today would make shooting unnecessary. He telephoned for police assistance, which arrived rapidly, and on Sir Garrard's instructions, a police marksman shot her. Unfortunately, the bullet lodged in her spine, disabling her but not killing her; Winston Taylor and "Yank" Miller at once closed in, and from short range put the animal out of her misery.

The noise of the first shot frightened Cæsar, who ran away and took refuge in an outhouse, "Yank" Miller following and quickly shutting the door on him. A trapping box was set up outside and baited with meat; and when the outhouse door was opened, Cæsar walked straight into it, and was soon returned to his den unharmed.

After the excitement of the lions' escape, winter calm returned to Cobtree until it was time to open up once more, for the Zoo's 24th season. The naturalists Armand and Michaela Denis were billed as the main attraction — they were famous for their wildlife programmes on B.B.C. Television, and Michaela for her book "A Leopard in My Lap" — but at the last minute they were called away to America; Richard Hearne was again in Australia (though he sent his best wishes), and Elsie and Doris Waters were busy rehearsing a new T.V. show.

Sir Garrard thus had a rather less renowned party than usual to introduce on March 24th, 1957, which was a pity, since the crowd, drawn by fine weather (the opening date was a week later than usual), was much larger than it had been the previous year. There was a legal luminary, Mr. Justice Hallett, Richard Hearne's wife, Yvonne Ortner and their two daughters, Cetra and Sarah, a well known local resident Mrs. Gordon Larking, and to perform the opening ceremony, the Mayor of Maidstone, Alderman Leslie Wallis, who was accompanied by Mrs. Wallis. In his speech, Alderman Wallis said that he was one of few Mayors of Maidstone who had ever had the High Sheriff of Kent (a position to which Sir Garrard had been appointed the previous year) as a member of the Council over which he presided. The High Sheriff was most respectful of the Mayoral Office, he went on, and it had never been necessary to call him to order.

A pair of lions in one of the new cages.

It was a privilege, said His Worship, to be allowed to open the Zoo, which had brought pleasure to so many people, and which played such an important role in keeping Maidstone on the map.

The usual conducted tour of the Zoo followed the Mayor's speech; it included a look at Nelson, a new leopard, and a spell at the dog track where Mr. Pastry's presence was greatly missed. The platform party also watched "Yank" Miller feed the lions, and had a look at some of the spring's new births, which included another Teddy Bear — not twins this time.

In June there was another new arrival — an Axis deer whose mother rejected it. It was bottle fed by several of the keepers, who named it Bambi, and survived to join the herd when it grew up. But there were not many new purchases from now on, for animal prices had soared since the war, and except for bears, were, on average over twice what they had been when Tyrwhitt-Drake opened his Zoo.

A female Asian elephant cost about £800 in 1957, so it is not surprising that Daisy was never replaced; a tiger cost £500 and a leopard £100 or more. Bear prices had remained relatively stable for a very good reason: bears are expensive to feed, they are extremely strong and difficult to handle, and they consequently require exceptionally substantial and secure accommodation.

Despite the relatively small number of new animals, Cobtree looked set for another successful season, when in June disaster struck the community, and attendance figures plummeted. There was a major outbreak of polio in Maidstone, causing widespread public alarm. People avoided contact with others as much as possible, even on their way to and from work, they did their shopping as quickly as they could, and even family gatherings and celebrations were cancelled. The swimming baths were closed, and outings and meetings of all kinds were called off or postponed.

Everywhere trade suffered: the shopkeepers of the town had a terrible season, and although on June 20th Sir Garrard issued a statement to the

"Yank" Miller feeding the sea lions.

Mother and child.

press saying that the Zoo was not affected by the outbreak, had not closed, and had no plans to do so, attendance figures recovered only slowly as the epidemic died down. Sadly, it had cost many local children their lives.

That the Zoo survived relatively unscathed, was undoubtedly due in part to the skill and loyalty of Sir Garrard's staff. There were, of course, numerous comings and goings, particularly of the girls who came straight from school and found zoo life too hard for them. But most of the staff were inspired by a love of animals, and a sense of personal loyalty to Sir Garrard and women such as Enid Basnett, Flossie Rayfield and Thelma Cornelius gave Cobtree years of unfailing service.

Many of the male staff lived in cottages on the estate, married and brought up families there, and spent the greater part of their working lives in Tyrwhitt-Drake's service. Often, at specially busy times, their wives and, during school holidays, their older children, glad of a little extra pocket money, would rally round and help to keep things going, manning the kiosks where refreshments for humans and animals were sold, and fetching and carrying; indeed, some of the women became personalities in their own right. One such was the wife of Jack Mathers, who looked after the heavy hoofed animals. As Madame Zara she was installed in an old caravan and enjoyed great success as a fortune teller. When not busy, she made cups of tea, liberally laced with Nestlés Milk, which are still remembered today by former members of the staff.

Jack was also Cobtree's mole catcher. Moles were often a problem, and so of course, as with most zoos, were rats and mice, especially at harvest time, when, driven from the fields, they sought new homes elsewhere. Poisons could not be used to control them, in case one of the animals ate a poisoned carcase, or, even more potentially serious, a visitor inadvertently handled one. Traps and smoke were used in the ceaseless campaign to keep pests down, and rats were shot.

Sir Garrard himself often roamed the Zoo just before darkness fell, shooting rats as they emerged to forage. On one occason at least, his aim failed him, for in the morning a keeper found an exotic pheasant dead in the aviary. She took it to Winston Taylor for examination, confirming that it had been alive and well the previous day. Taylor found the bird had indeed been in excellent health, but that it had suffered a fatal gunshot wound overnight. Sir Garrard made the best he could of things and had it for dinner.

The Final Years

A T 5.00 p.m. on the last Sunday in October 1957 the Zoo closed for another winter. A disappointing season ended for the staff with a disappointing bonus. It had long been Sir Garrard's custom to pay his workers a bonus at the end of each summer, the amount being based on the number of visitors received. This year, as some compensation for the poor pay out he offered everyone a Cobtree duck for Christmas (he had always been prepared to sell one on request). Most accepted, but some, including Thelma Cornelius declined. "I felt I couldn't eat one of my own charges", she said.

A substantial investment in new buildings and equipment was now well overdue; but at the age of 76 Sir Garrard was increasingly reluctant to undertake more than routine replacement and refurbishment, so the permanent staff occupied themselves with painting and minor repairs: Mr. Court, a local carpenter, was called in for anything beyond Cobtree's own resources.

The 1958 season was inaugurated on a cold day in April by Sir Malcolm Sargent, who said that the Cobtree animals could count themselves as very lucky: they had warm, dry quarters in which to live, and had to worry neither about where the next meal was coming from nor about the danger of themselves being someone else's next lunch. He was supported on the platform by old friends Richard Hearne and Yvonne Ortner, as well as by Sir Alfred Bossom, M.P., Lady Mallet, Professor Cave, Miss G. Stabies, Miss M. Noakes and the Mayor and Mayoress of Maidstone, Alderman and Mrs. S. J. Lyle.

Despite the freezing wind, a good crowd had assembled to watch the proceedings and hear Sir Malcolm, who was already well known to many people not particularly interested in classical music for his regular appearances on T.V. as conductor of the Last Night of the Proms. Sir Garrard's guests, as on some previous occasions, had seen something of the Zoo before the opening ceremony, but afterwards they went to see two lions, Sonhrab and Rustum, which had been found in the Southern plain of Somaliland, now the Somali Republic, and presented to the Zoo by two Somali Scouts; and they also had a look at a new collection of macaws and parrots which had recently arrived from British Guiana, now Guyana.

When the guests had retired to the Manor for the statutory tea, the paying visitors hurried to see Martha the second, who now weighed seventeen stone — an outstanding example of middle age spread which may have made some onlookers a little thoughtful. Such examples of animal obesity clearly made zoologists thoughtful too; at that time, visitors to Cobtree, and most other Zoos, were not only encouraged to bring bread crusts from home with which to feed inmates, but for the same purpose could buy bags of apples, nuts and stale biscuits from kiosks strategically located throughout the grounds. The feeding of only a few animals was prohibited; now it is almost universally forbidden. Even so, no cases are recorded of any Cobtree inmate dying or becoming ill as a result of eating unsuitable food offered to it by a visitor.

The season which followed was uneventful; there were no escapes, no unusual births. But attendance kept up well, with no epidemics to keep visitors away, and the café, now in the hands of Mr. Avery, did good business. When there was a rush, a small shop nearby would be opened to sell cakes, soft drinks and tea, which was made on a gas ring used in winter time for boiling up potato peelings and cereals to make a warm mash for the monkeys.

Some time during the year "Yank" Miller died. He had lived with his dog in a cottage on the estate since his arrival and had looked after the big cats well. But their number had declined — many of the lions were now too old to breed — and no replacement for him was engaged.

Closure for the winter came at the end of October, and the Zoo settled down to its usual programme of cleaning and repairs. By now, the need for replacement was very evident in places. The path leading from the carnivores enclosure to Pets' Corner had been worn smooth by many feet; the shingle surface was quite glossy, and particularly difficult for people with steel shoe protectors to negotiate without slipping. Luckily Sir Garrard was never faced with a claim for damages from anyone unlucky enough to suffer injury by falling on it, but large numbers of impertinent children were reduced to hysterics at the sight of their elders and betters desperately trying to keep their balance as they tottered along it.

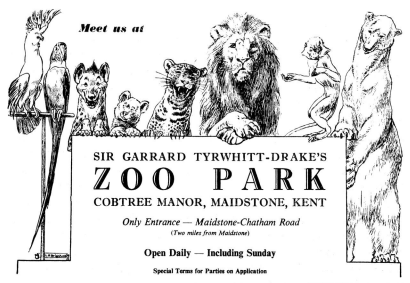

Meet us at

SIR GARRARD TYRWHITT-DRAKE'S
ZOO PARK
COBTREE MANOR, MAIDSTONE, KENT

Only Entrance — Maidstone-Chatham Road
(Two miles from Maidstone)

Open Daily — Including Sunday

Special Terms for Parties on Application

Please reply to:
30 HIGH STREET, MAIDSTONE
Phone: Maidstone 2774

February 24th, 1959.

Miss L. F. Rayfield,
12, Darnley Close,
Strood, Rochester.

Madam,

      Sir Garrard Tyrwhitt-Drake has asked me to
write and enquire how you are, and when you are likely to
return to work. He of course does not want you to come
back before you are well enough to do so, but they are so
short handed in the Zoo. Will you let him know.

      I am getting you a three-month Season Ticket
to date from February 28th, so please do not get another
monthly ticket, - I believe your present one expires on Feb.
27th.

                Yours truly,

                              .Secretary.

An encouraging get well soon letter to Flossie Rayfield.

Time honoured procedures were followed as old and virtually life expired equipment was once again renovated: a method borrowed from the world of circus was employed for repainting the lions' ancient cages without removing their inhabitants. After the cages had been washed down, a strong wooden board, known as a slide-board, was inserted between the bars at the front and into a slot in the rear wall fashioned to receive it. Painting then proceeded in the half of the cage without a lion in it until the work was finished, when the board was withdrawn, and the lion persuaded to change ends. The board was then pushed in again and work resumed in the second half of the cage.

Albertina the sea lion was released from her enclosure during the day now that no members of the public were roaming round the grounds, and thoroughly enjoyed her freedom. She particularly liked chasing the chickens which were usually pecking around near her pool, and was entranced when the weather turned cold in January, and for a while there was snow on the ground. The Cobtree staff were not so pleased, of course: water pipes froze, as did the lake, and all the daily chores became more difficult to perform. The animals did not suffer, however, and ended the winter in fine shape.

Sir Garrard was not so lucky. He was unwell for much of the winter, and unable to take part in the ceremonies to mark the start of the 1959 season. In his absence the advance publicity for opening day had been much lower-key than usual, and as a result the attendance was down on that of previous years. Lady Edna took his place on the platform, supported only by the Tyrwhitt-Drake's old friends Richard Hearne and Yvonne Ortner and their daughters Cetra and Sarah, and by Winston Taylor, who was now designated Zoo Manager. Hearne brought greetings from Sir Garrard, who said that he was very sorry and sad that he could not be with the party that day, but hoped that everyone would have a good time. Hearne went on to tell the crowd that it was the seventeenth time that he had played a part in festivities at Cobtree, either as himself or as Mr. Pastry (and sometimes as both). It was indeed, tangible evidence of how much he and his family loved the place.

After declaring the Zoo open, Hearne led the small platform party away to meet a group of children from Dene Park School at Shipbourne, who had been specially invited for the afternoon; adopting his role as Mr. Pastry, he led them to Pets' Corner and introduced them to many of the more cuddly inmates before continuing the traditional first day tour. No new animals had been purchased during the winter, but as usual there

The last Opening Day. Lady Edna is at the microphone, behind her stands Richard Hearne in his famous rôle as Mr. Pastry, his wife Yvonne Ortner and his two daughters Cetra and Sarah.

were some new babies to see, and old friends like Gert the elephant and Martha the chimp to visit. Then it was off to the races at the dog track, with Mr. Pastry causing chaos, while Reg Yardley endeavoured to control the hare, and together with Arthur Carter and the girls from Pets' Corner, struggled to box the excited dogs before each of the usual five races, and to catch them afterwards. Sir Garrard was able to join his guests at tea in the Manor at the end of the afternoon, and was doubtless happy to learn that all had gone well, despite the small size of the platform party and the reduced attendance.

Admission charges were unchanged for the new season, and at a time of steady price rises a visit to Cobtree now represented outstandingly good value for money. A day at the Zoo still cost only 2/- (10p) for adults and

1/- (5p) for children; car parking was 6d. (2½p) per day, and the price of the attractions in the Zoo remained extremely low: a pony ride for example was also only 6d. An afternoon's motor racing at Brands Hatch on the other hand cost 5/- (25p), with another 5/- to park a car.

The summer was warm and dry — so dry in fact that in July Maidstone Waterworks Company, of which Sir Garrard was still a Director, complained in a public announcement about the poor response to its recent appeal for economy in the use of water. It went on to impose a ban on the use of water for garden hoses, washing cars and similar non-domestic purposes, and added a threat that if this did not prove effective in reducing consumption, water might have to be cut off at night. The threat was not implemented, but the ban on hoses and car washing continued for weeks, well into September.

As a result, Sir Garrard's yellow Rolls Royce had to be washed with buckets of water; but the drought did not otherwise affect Cobtree, and the warm sunny days brought good crowds to the Zoo. At about the same time that the restrictions on the use of water were announced, a Capuchin, or ring-tailed monkey, gave birth to a baby daughter which, however, she immediately rejected. Winston Taylor at once adopted the tiny creature, which was christened Minnie, and with help from most of the staff, bottle-fed it until it could be weaned on to its adult diet of fruit, insects and eggs. Flossie Rayfield's sister Sarah knitted some little woolly coats for it, to compensate for the lack of a mother's warmth, and remembers that when it was already three months old, its size was that of a 7½ inch doll.

Minnie was to be Cobtree's last birth; Sir Garrard was now 78 years old, and was no longer so robust as in former years. In September he called a press conference at Cobtree, and announced that "with deep regret and sadness" he had decided to close the Zoo at the end of the season.

If there had been an heir to take over, Sir Garrard might well have reached a different decision; he had kept animals for over sixty years, and as he said in announcing the closure, he would miss them greatly, "especially the lions, which have always been my favourites". But he felt the need for a quieter and more peaceful life, and it would not have been his way to leave responsibilty for everything to Winston Taylor while continuing to live at the Manor, within sight and sound of the Zoo. So he announced the end, and to minimise the death agony, set the closing date earlier than usual, at the beginning instead of the end of October.

The weeks which followed were both sad and busy. The lives of many members of the staff, and not a few members of the public, were closely

Winston Taylor with Minnie, the monkey whose life he saved.

bound to the Zoo; Reg Yardley and "Captain" Gates had spent a large part of their working lives in Sir Garrard's service, Mrs. Hussey had looked after the entrance kiosk since early in the war, and Miss K. Ottewill, though rarely seen by visitors, had been Sir Garrard's secretary since the Zoo opened. She did not work at Cobtree, but in an office at 30 High Street, Maidstone, where she handled all the great mass of paperwork involved in running the Zoo.

Among members of the public, none can have been more affected than Martin Hammond. A tall, quiet man who always wore a trilby hat, he had started coming to the Zoo many years earlier to study the animals, and had just continued coming. He came every Sunday, and grew to know

"Captain" Gates with his charge, apparently straight from the beauty parlour.

Jack Bourne painting one of the lions' cages using the dividing board technique.

the staff, and they him; he would help them out with odd jobs, and they would give him cups of tea at break times; he was there on the final day.

Everyone had to adjust to a new and unknown future and at the same time the staff had to make speedy arrangements for the disposal of the animal collection. When the gates of Maidstone Zoo at Cobtree closed for the last time on the evening of Sunday, 4th October, 1959, most of the animals were still there, but some of the staff had already left, and an era had come to an end.

When the final visitors had gone, Winston Taylor remained, together with Reg Yardley, Arthur Carter, "Captain" Gates, Flossie Rayfield, Thelma Cornelius, Bunnie Hazel, who had only recently joined the Zoo, and Mrs. Hussey. Bunnie Hazel left very soon, and Gates, Yardley and Mrs. Hussey retired, though they continued to live on the estate, Gates until he died, aged 75, in 1963. Thus the final disposal of the animals and the closing down of the facilities was left to Taylor, Carter, Flossie Rayfield and Thelma Cornelius.

Some of the animals were presented to other Zoos, and plaques were erected near their new homes explaining where they had come from. Gert the elephant was purchased by Sir Billy Butlin, who had a soft spot for elephants, and went to live at Butlin's at Pwllheli in North Wales, where she was renamed Gertie. She was given a paddock near the headland, and looked after by a keeper known as Indian Ram, who had accommodation next door to her. He grew very attached to her, and during the season took her on daily walks through the camp, with a scheduled stop near the fruit stall where holiday makers would regale her with her favourite food.

Later Gertie was moved to Butlin's at Skegness, possibly to replace another elephant there which had died of grief after the death of its keeper. Indian Ram did not accompany her, a keeper known as Steve taking his place. She was re-christened for a third time when she arrived in Lincolnshire, henceforth being known as Gertrude which seems a very formal name for such a friendly elephant.

Opposite.

A line up of staff and friends shortly before closure. On the extreme left is Bunnie Hazel, standing by the goat are Thelma Cornelius and Winston Taylor, and next to him is Flossie Rayfield.

Sadly, she did not have very long in which to enjoy the famous bracing air of Skegness, for she died tragically not many months after her arrival. Steve often took her for a walk through the camp before the guests were up, and one morning while out with him she decided to have a dip in one of the camp swimming pools. Unfortunately, the base was not strong enough to support her weight, and she fell through it, and quickly became jammed in the broken foundations. Steve was unable to hold her head above water while the pool was drained, and so poor Gert drowned after a life in which she had given pleasure to tens of thousands of children and adults and harmed no one.

Arthur Carter found employment with Southend Borough Council, and took the second chimp named Martha, Rinty, a Himalayan black bear, and a collection of monkeys with him to Essex, where, under his care, they were installed in one of the local parks. The axis deer, of which there were five when the Zoo closed, together with the hog deer and the Nilghai antelopes, were bought by John Aspinall who put them in his zoos at Port Lymne and Bekesbourne, where their descendants can still be seen today. The axis deer in particular have prospered in his care; the herd has grown to number more than sixty.

The aquarium was soon emptied: the cold water fish were put back in the lake at Cobtree where they normally spent the winter, while the tropicals were returned, as they had been at the end of every season since the aquarium opened, to their owners, the London Zoo. Jack, one of the lions, was now very old, and would not have survived a move, so he was put down, while Minnie, the Zoo's last baby, went to adorn Mr. Fox's pet shop in Herne Bay, where she was definitely not for sale.

When it was all over, Winston Taylor left for Belle Vue Zoo, Manchester, taking with him a few parrots. The remainder stayed at Cobtree, and for Lady Edna's pleasure, Sir Garrard had a small new parrot house built for them near the Manor.

Sir Garrard also kept his llamas and his herd of Royal Cream ponies — handsome relics of the great animal collection he had once owned. He lived on at Cobtree for another five years, and died in October 1964 at the age of 83. The ponies were then presented to Whipsnade Zoo, where their successors remain, though the prefix "Royal" has been dropped from their name. Some were sent to Regents Park Zoo, to take visitors on carriage drives round the grounds.

Thus, after echoing to the sounds of exotic beasts for 59 years, Cobtree finally fell silent.

The Present Day

SIR GARRARD rests in a modest grave in Maidstone Cemetery. At each side of his headstone are a pair of stone lions which were originally on the gate posts at the private entrance to Cobtree Manor. Lions were always his favourite animals, it is appropriate that they should mark his resting place.

He left a very complex will, the end result of which is that the estate and manor are under the management of Maidstone Borough Council "For the benefit of the people of Maidstone". Lady Edna lived in the manor house until her death in 1992 at the age of 90 and the future of the house is still under discussion.

Great progress has been made however on the development of the estate. Part of the farmland to the south of Forstal Road has been developed as the Museum of Kent Life, and this is well worth a visit. The land bordering the A229 Chatham Road, where once hundreds of cars and coaches were parked, and whence the train carried visitors to the Zoo entrance, has been developed as a public golf course. It is possible, by crossing the golf course, to enter the area of the Zoo by the original public gate. But a safer access is by the country park and nature trail into which much of the area has been developed.

To reach the country park, leave Maidstone by the A229 Chatham Road and at the roundabout giving access to the M20 turn left onto the road signposted Aylesford. The entrance to the country park is about half a mile from the roundabout on the right hand side. The bus service to Aylesford passes the entrance.

In the park, memorial gates have been erected to acknowledge the debt the people of Maidstone owe to Sir Garrard and Lady Edna Tyrwhitt-Drake. The dedication on the gates reads.

<table>
<tr><td>

This
Parkland Garden
was created for
the benefit of
the people of
Maidstone

</td><td>

To commemorate
the benefactions
bestowed on the town
by Sir Garrard and Lady
Tyrwhitt-Drake
1881-1966   1902-1992

</td></tr>
</table>

Although little of the Zoo now remains, it is still possible to look into the elephant house, which has been refurbished and is at present being used as a store, and to walk in Wolf Wood. There are still moles at Cobtree, but the elephants and the wolves and the crowds who came to see them are long gone. Only perhaps in the minds of those who have read this book, and the memories of those who knew and loved the place, does the dream which Tyrwhitt-Drake turned into reality live on.

A former pony field shelter, now refurbished as a picnic area.

The refurbished Elephant House. Access for visitors was by the door below the sign; there was a similar one on the other side of the building.

The rear of the Elephant House showing the residents' entrance.

Appendix

The following list of Zoo residents has been compiled from the lists published by Sir Garrard in the Zoo Guide from time to time. It claims to be neither comprehensive nor complete but only a guide to the animals that were on view during the life of the Zoo.

MAMMALS

Agoutis

Alpacas

Armadillos

Badgers

Blackbuck

Bears, Black Canadian
    Brown European
    Himalayan
    Malayan
    Polar
    Sloth

Bisons

Baboons, Chacma
    Guinea

Camels, Arabian
    Bactrian

Cattle, Dexter
    Highland

Capybaras

Caracals

Cheetahs

Chimpanzees

Civet Cats

Coatis

Coypus

Deer, Axis
    Chinese Water
    Fallow
    Hog
    Kashmere

Deer, Muntjac
    Pere David
    Red

Dogs, Beagle
    Husky

Donkeys, North American Miniature

Dingoes

Elephants

Ferrets

Foxes, Arabian
    Red
    Silver

Goats, Nubian
    Royal White

Gnus

Guinea Pigs

Hyenas, Spotted
    Striped

Ibexes, Caucasian

Jackals

Kangaroo

Kinkajous

Lemurs

Leopards

Lions

Llamas

Lynxs

Marmots

Mice

Monkeys, Black Spider
       Bonnet
       Calatrix
       Capuchin
       Green
       Macaque
       Mandrill
       Mangabey
       Rhesus
       Woolly
Nilgais
Otters
Peccaries
Polecats
Ponies, Royal Cream
       Shetland
Porcupines, Crested
       Malayan
Pumas
Rabbits
Racoons
Racoon Dogs
Rats, Black
       Giant Pouched
       White
Seals
Sea Lions
Sheep, Barbary
       Mouflon
       Soay
Squirrels
Swine, Wild
Tigers, Bengal
       Chinese
Viscachas
Wallabies
Wolves, Coyote
       European
       Indian
       Timber

Yaks
Zebras
Zebus

BIRDS

Black Cuckoos
Budgerigars
Chinese Blue Magpies
Cranes, Demoiselle
       Sarus
Cockatoos, Bare-eyed
       Leadbetters
       Lemon Crested (small)
       Lemon Crested (large)
       Roseate
       Slender Beak
Crows, Jackdaw
       Jay
       Raven
       Rook
Doves, Barbary
       Ringed
       Turtle
Eagles, African Sea
       American Bald-headed
       Golden
       Spotted
Emus
Finches, Cut Throat
       Fire
       Java Sparrow
       Whydahs
       Zebra
Geese, Canadian
       Chinese
       Muscovy
       Spurwing
       Upland
Golden Orioles
Guinea Fowl, Helmeted

Hawks, Buzzard
      Kestrel
Herons
Kites
Macaws, Blue and Yellow
      Brown Fronted
      Hyacinth
      Illiger
      Red and Green
Owls, Barn
      Eagle
      Little
      Tawny
      Virginia Eagle
Paraqueets, Ring Necked
Mynahs
Parrots, Golden Amazon
      Green Amazon
      Grey
Pea Fowl, Black Winged
      Common
      White
Penguins, Black Footed
Pelicans
Pheasants, Amherst
      Amherst × Gold
      Chir
      Golden
      Monauls
      Reeves
      Ring-necked
      Silver
      Swinhoe
Pigeons, Ice
      Modena
      Tumbler
      Wood
Poultry, Bantams
      Frizzles
      Old English Game
      Silkies
      Yokohama

Rheas, Grey
      White
Seabirds, Gulls
      Gannet
      Razorbill
Storks, Black and White
Swans, Black
      Hooper
      White
Toucans
Turkeys, Blue
      Bronze
      Brush
Vultures, African
      Caracara
      King

FISH

Gold, sub varieties
Orfe
Perch
Roach
Rudd
Tropical, Angel
      Mexican Swordtail
      Moon
      Paradise
      Rainbow

REPTILES

Lizards, Brown
      Green
Salamanders
Snakes, Glass
      Grass
Terrapins
Tortoises

Together with a range of farm and domestic animals.

Acknowledgements

I am indebted to the following for the use of photographs

P. Back — pages 15 and 28

T. Davies — page 20

R. J. Gander — page 127

M. Hammond — pages 25, 37, 38, 45, 49 (bottom), 56, 110 (top) and 121

Ms Hammond — page 86

D. Jarman — pages 32, 40, 55, 64, 79, 81 (right), 82, 100 and 130

Kent Messenger Group — pages 93, 114, 120, 129 and 132

Ms Love — page 42

A. Madle — page 35

Maidstone Museum — page 12

E. Simmonds — pages 53, 76, 81 (left), 94, 95 and 131

M. White — page 143

R. White — pages 4, 6, 22, 36, 44, 49 (top), 62, 68, 70, 71, 72, 73, 75, 78, 84, 90, 91, 98, 105, 111 and 115

Ms Wilding — pages 103 and 119

COVER DESIGN BY NEIL HARRIS

Sir Hugh Garrard Tyrwhitt-Drake — one of a special kind.